Race and the Renewal of the Church

CHRISTIAN PERSPECTIVES
ON SOCIAL PROBLEMS

Gayraud S. Wilmore, *General Editor*

Race
and the Renewal
of the Church

by

WILL D. CAMPBELL

Philadelphia
THE WESTMINSTER PRESS

COPYRIGHT © MCMLXII, BY W. L. JENKINS

All rights reserved—no part of this book may be reproduced in any form without permission in writing from the publisher, except by a reviewer who wishes to quote brief passages in connection with a review in magazine or newspaper.

Scripture quotations from the Revised Standard Version of the Bible are copyright, 1946 and 1952, by the Division of Christian Education of the National Council of Churches, and are used by permission.

LIBRARY OF CONGRESS CATALOG CARD NO. 62–12146

PRINTED IN THE UNITED STATES OF AMERICA

Contents

Foreword

THIS BOOK IS ONE OF SEVERAL TO APPEAR DURING THE next few years in a series entitled Christian Perspectives on Social Problems. This is an attempt to meet a challenge from an exceedingly robust minority of laymen for brief, readable analyses of cultural problems from a theological perspective. It is intended to help them *think theologically* about some of the exasperatingly difficult problems of society, both the issues relating to life in America and those linking this nation to the destiny of the world.

Recent researches on family life have found laymen obsessed with "loving, happy relations" in the family, with child-rearing and personal problems of status and adjustment, but with little comprehension of how private troubles bisect public issues. This curious fascination with selfhood to the neglect of neighborhood is not, however, a universal malaise of Protestantism. A minority, perhaps, but a minority that refuses to be lightly regarded by ecclesiastical officialdom, is demanding to know the meaning of events of our day for the Christian faith and to demonstrate the critical and renewing power of faith in secular society.

It is to these doughty men and women that the several volumes of the Christian Perspectives on Social Problems series are directed, and it is hoped that they not only will

1

make for an unsettling reading experience but will provide stimulating material for small-group study and discussion. To that end, questions for discussion are appended to each of the books as starters for fruitful controversy.

Will Campbell, the author of the present volume, is a pioneer trouble shooter in areas of racial tension. He has seen at first hand most serious crises in race relations in both the North and the South, in an advisory and consultative capacity for the National Council of Churches.

RACE AND THE RENEWAL OF THE CHURCH is wrought out of the frustrations and loneliness of one who has borne the brunt of the churches' witness in this greatest of all social problems. It is an angry but a compassionate book. Its anger is muted by a deep sense of the tragedy of sin with which the whole struggle is suffused and by its realism about the necessary means by which the church can break through to the segregationist within its own ranks. Above the pessimism concerning the witness of white Protestantism for racial justice there is here an overarching spirit of compassion for the fractured community of mankind and a confidence in the victory which God can bring out of the weakness of his church.

This first volume of the series raises a variety of perplexing questions about how the church should proceed in its social witness beyond the particular issue of racial discrimination. The positions taken here do not necessarily represent either the official posture of the National Council of Churches or the viewpoint of other writers in the series. Each of the authors will state his own case. Will Campbell ably presents his in these pages.

GAYRAUD S. WILMORE

Pittsburgh, Pennsylvania

Chapter I

Are *We* Still the Church?

IN MANY PARTS OF THE WORLD, OUR TIME HAS AL-
ready been labeled "the post-Christian era." This is simply
one measure of the fact that for many people the church
has become irrelevant. It has waited too long to carry out
its mandate, and to a large part of the world, what we
Christians do from here on out really does not matter
very much.

Christendom came very close to gaining the whole
world. It is now, or so say its critics, dangerously close to
losing its own soul. In no area more crucial to the future
of the church is this more true than in the area of race
relations.

In this context, to write a book on Christian race relations is not only presumptuous; it is downright ludi-
crous. And yet, if we believe the world will not find
a better way, we must believe that someday it will turn
back to the church. That day, however, has not yet
arrived.

Let us begin by saying that our concern in this little
book is not how to reform the world for freedom, justice,
and democracy. If this was ever the responsibility of the
church, the opportunity has passed us by. Exciting efforts
are being made in this direction, but not within our ranks.
The church has abdicated its position of leadership. If it

3

ever was or should have been, it is no longer the initiator or prime mover of social reform.

In Africa and Asia the leadership is found today in the tidal wave of nationalism sweeping those two continents and carrying their peoples toward political and economic independence. In America, the most promising and exciting developments in human relations are taking place, not in the churches, but in government.

The church might have influenced these developments by being true to its own nature. It might have determined their success or failure, but it failed to act. It waited until government took the initiative to rescue human rights. And today when the church acts in the human relations field, it follows government or political authority. It imitates the action of the state or it confirms such action with a pious benediction. Moreover, when it has acted, the church has adopted largely a humanitarian approach. Its voice has been too often an echo of the cry for law and order, democracy, the rights of man, human dignity, constitutional process, the public schools.

These things are good, but are they the most basic, most distinctive, concern of the church? In these pages, we will try to determine whether our concern is not something far more basic and more radical than anything the state has said. In the process we will attempt to establish that the church's failure in the racial crisis has been not functional but organic, not sociological but theological. In effect, we have been asking the wrong questions. Instead of demanding, What can the Christian *do* to improve race relations? we should be asking, What must the Christian *be*? As the body of Christ, the church first of all must be the redeemed community. Then will it be empowered to redeem the world, and not before. The sin of the church is not that it has not reformed society, but that it has not realized self-renewal. Its sin is that it has not repented. Without repentance there cannot be renewal.

For the health of our own souls, it might have been better if the Supreme Court had not ruled favorably in 1954 on the subject of race. It might have been better if there had been no executive orders from the White House on fair employment, integration of the Armed Services, and open occupancy in public housing. Then we would have been forced to speak, if we spoke at all, from the vantage point of the Christian gospel. We would have been required to say, Thus saith the Lord! Not, Thus saith the law!

In South Africa, where the full force of law and government is on the side of segregation and discrimination, when churchmen speak they do not echo the state. They cannot fall back upon patriotic and legalistic arguments to urge their people to do what is right. Those Christians who have spoken as the voice of God have often been deposed, arrested for treason, subjected to continuing legal and political harassment. But their message has been strong and clear. They blow a lonely horn, but for them the church has real identity.

Within recent years some American churchmen have insisted that there is no such thing as *Christian* race relations, that our message on this subject is not in the least a particular and peculiar one, and that we are, therefore, justified in taking our cue from the social sciences or from the state. But is this really the case? And if there are indeed no *Christian* race relations, is it not because the Christian message on race is the same as the Christian message on every problem of human life? We shall develop this more fully in a later chapter.

Why is the church concerned about race? First, let us look at the usual reasons.

The church is *not* motivated by fear of reprisals by the nonwhite peoples of the world, although we must recognize that such reprisals are a distinct possibility. Both the Christian doctrine of sin and the most rudimentary acquaintance with man's nature make it sentimental and unrealistic to suppose that people who have been oppressed and exploited for centuries will reach independence and equality filled with love and forgiveness and free of any vindictiveness, prejudice, or animosity.

The Christian understanding of sin makes it highly probable that our generation will see white children marched into gas chambers by dark masters, clutching their little toys to their breasts in Auschwitz fashion. It could see senile whites forced to dig their own mass grave by a heavily pigmented Eichmann. Even a casual glance at history makes this just as probable as does the Christian understanding of human sin and the nature of man. Americans are not inclined to take this possibility seriously, for in this country the lack of superior, sophisticated Negro leadership is not acute. On a world scale it is serious, especially at a time when one miscalculation in Moscow or Washington, too much vodka in the Kremlin or too much bourbon beside the Potomac, could bring forth a day of blinding flashes and lethal explosions which would completely redraw the present power alignments. Great nations would be as nothing. New emerging nations would be great powers.

Alan Paton, in his poignant novel about life in South Africa, *Cry, the Beloved Country* (Charles Scribner's Sons, 1950), had the elderly native preacher comment: "My greatest fear is that by the time the whites have turned to loving, my people will have turned to hating." Recent developments in Paton's country, in the Congo, in the United States, and in other parts of the world, have already proved that his fear is not unfounded.

But this cannot be our concern. What may happen when black people rather than white people are "on top" is irrelevant to our task. Certainly the Christian is concerned any time brother is killing brother, but there is nothing distinctively Christian in being exercised about the fact that you may be the Abel rather than the Cain. As followers of Jesus Christ we cannot say, "Let us be good to nonwhites; otherwise they may eliminate us."

Nor is our concern with international relations. There can be no question about the injurious effect of our policies and practices at home on our standing and prestige abroad. A riot in New Orleans, Little Rock, or Levittown is news throughout Africa, and the bombing of a Jewish temple in America may well be welcome propaganda material in Moscow. But this is still not a sufficient reason for concern by the church.

Nor can our concern be the salvaging of our overseas mission programs. One denomination that gives $18,-500,000 a year to foreign missions and $30,000 for race relations (a ratio of 640 to 1) is beginning to take African nationals into local congregations because of what it may do for the missions program. But the African people will not be deceived, and it is doubtful whether our desire for better missionary statistics is any more pleasing to God than is the hue and cry of the real estate broker about depressing "property values."

Since none of these is reason enough for the church's concern, we must now say that this is really not a book on race. Nor can it accurately be described as a treatise on the church's position with respect to race, or an essay on the Bible and race. It is nothing more than an effort to discuss something about which the Bible said nothing, which the early church ignored, and which the historic church has never recognized as a valid concept within its own life, but which, nevertheless, has plagued the church for ages and is today the most serious issue it has to face.

Within orthodox Christianity, when race has been dealt with—even to the point of organizing segregated churches—it has generally been under the cloak of some other question: local autonomy, expediency, harmony within the fellowship. Seldom has it been under the bold banner of race per se. And where this has been the case in the historic church, the majority thinking has insisted that recognition of race to the point of segregation is not in accord with the true faith, but is at best a malignant dissidence or schism, and at worst a perilous heresy.

Because the Christian faith neither recognized nor tolerated the idea of race from its earliest beginning, a Christian in the field of race relations does not speak as a member of a racial group. Because the church did not begin as a racially segregated (or integrated) institution but rather as an institution in which race was irrelevant, the Christian does not speak as a white man, a Negro, an Oriental, or an Occidental.

Instead, the Christian speaks as a member of a community which has never asked any question save the one concerning redemption. What do you think of Jesus? The Christian, therefore, speaks as the offspring of a "peculiar family," so strange as to be called a *tertium genus,* a third race, a people neither Jew or Greek, bond nor free, embracing master and slave alike, king and liege equally, asking only one question of each: Who, do you believe, is this man who is called the Christ? But despite the christening of the church as the third race, it has not been faithful to its name. Born above race, we have been attracted to the world of races. We have been a stubborn and stiff-necked people and again and again we have forgotten the name we bear.

To be sure, the church as an institution has made some progress in recent decades. When we compare the church of today with the church thirty or forty years ago, there is a clear line of advance. But as far as race relations are concerned, when we compare ourselves to such secular agencies as sports organizations, education, government, the Armed Forces, and even industry and the labor movement, we must ask ourselves whether we really are not even more backward now than we were three decades ago.

For example, in organized sports a few years ago Negroes were not allowed to participate, but they were permitted to be spectators, although the stands were segregated in some sections of the country. In the churches the same was true. Negroes could generally attend white congregations but usually could not join or participate in the full life of the church. Now, in industry, government, the Armed Services, and organized sports, Negroes are beginning to participate. This, however, has not come about in the churches, except on very rare occasions. True, there are a few more interracial congregations than previously, and some denominations on the national level have begun to employ a few Negroes in executive positions. But for the most part, there is still a white church and a Negro church, just as there once was white baseball and Negro baseball. Relatively speaking, the church is farther behind than ever.

We have now come to the whole point of this rather painful disclosure. We must ask ourselves, earnestly and prayerfully, whether *we* are still the church. If we discover that God has turned to other vehicles, it will not be because he has left his people, but because the people have left God. The Temple of Israel was finally brought low, not because God had ceased to be the God of the people, but because the people had ceased to be the people of God; the Temple had become a market place and a symbol of national idolatry.

The church is not the church because of what man is and has done but because of what God is and has done through Christ. The first mark of the church is that it belongs to Christ. Yet we find ourselves speaking of "our church" and "their church," and of how "*they* seem to want to come to *our* church." As members of the body, we are clearly usurping the power that belongs only to the head of the body. These things are not ours to decide.

The Christian message on race relations is, "God was

in Christ reconciling the world to himself" (II Cor. 5:19). Throughout the New Testament, Christ's work of reconciliation re-establishes not only the father-son relationship but the brother-brother relationship. These are not two separate truths somehow related and requiring proper balance. Nor are they mutually related; they are one and the same truth. The New Testament writer who said "God was in Christ" said a few sentences earlier (v. 16), "From now on, therefore, we regard no one from a human point of view." This was to insist that those who are received into this fellowship, into the community of the redeemed, the church, are to be seen, not as they once were—Asians, Africans, Jews, Greeks, slave, free, male, female, not in any of these human categories or classifications—but in a new category or a new classification.

"Therefore, if any one is in Christ, he is a new creation; the old has passed away, behold, the new has come." (II Cor. 5:17.) Thus for the Christian to continue to place his brothers and sisters in Christ into the old classifications is for him to deny the faith he claims. It is precisely at this point—the denial of the faith in the name of the faith—that the church is most in danger of losing its life. For the apostle Paul, whose words we have just cited, continued: ". . . and entrusting to us the message of reconciliation" (II Cor. 5:19). But how can we preach the message of reconciliation if we are a living denial of it? If we deny that message of reconciliation entrusted to us, are we in fact still the church?

This question has many hazards. John Calvin said: "We have no right lightly to abandon the church because it is not perfect." Certainly all branches of the holy catholic church are subject to error and do err. Certainly all individual members of the corporate body are subject to sin and do sin. The church does not cease to be the church because it errs or because its members continue in sin. The institution may be able to neglect its mission and remain the church. But there is real doubt that it can both neglect its mission *and* deny its very nature and yet remain the church.

When the church excludes those who come crying for inclusion, confessing their sins, professing belief in the Lordship of Christ; when it views fellow believers through human categories and classifications, it is denying its nature. For the church, by nature, is inclusive and corporate. One cannot say, "I will live in fellowship with all who believe in the same Lord as I, provided they do not come from Philadelphia." Being from Philadelphia, being a white man or a Negro, is a human category, and, following the apostle Paul, "from now on . . . we regard no one from a human point of view" (II Cor. 5:16). There is now only one category for those who are Christ's, and we cannot arbitrarily rule otherwise. Race is a human category and is not one of the questions the church asks. Therefore, when we ask about the race of a fellow Christian, explicitly or implicitly, we are not being true to our nature as Christ's people.

The same truth holds when we evangelize according to racial neighborhoods or racial households. This is to neglect the true purpose of our mission. God has entrusted to us his message of reconciliation. When we withhold it, when we pass over a geographical locale because "they are not our people," we are neglecting or betraying our mission. God has created this new humanity, this new creation—the church—"to preach good news to the poor, . . . to proclaim release to the captives and recovering of sight to the blind, to set at liberty those who are oppressed, to proclaim the acceptable year of the Lord" (Luke 4:18–19, from Isa. 61:1–2). If the church regards people from a human point of view in the pursuit of this mission, it neglects the calling and the charge that its Lord has laid upon it.

Of course, the segregationist will say: "But I can love

the member of a minority group, I can have his welfare at heart, I can do all the good things one Christian might be expected to do for another and *still insist that he stay in a separate neighborhood, school, and church.*"

Two things must be said in answer to this. First of all, Christ left us no such freedom. The nature of the church denies us such a privilege. As members of the corporate body of Christ, we may not classify or categorize. "The eye cannot say to the hand, I have no need of you. . . . On the contrary, the parts of the body which seem to be weaker are indispensable." (I Cor. 12:21–22.) Thus, even if one could prove that a racial group or any other human category is inferior, low in morals, lazy, shiftless, lower in intelligence, given to various weaknesses of character, the New Testament tells us that these are all excellent reasons for that group to be included.

The second thing that must be said to the segregationist who insists that he can love his brother and still restrict his freedom through a system of segregation is that this simply is not true. Who, having two children, can claim to love them equally if he puts one in a room— which he himself selects—gives that child the same toys, clothes, food, and medical care as the other child whom he has not restricted to an assigned room but has given the freedom of the house and grounds, including even the room assigned to the first child? The segregationist is often honest and sincere in his belief that he loves the minority person whom he restricts, but we may well question whether he really knows the meaning of love.

We must say, then, frankly recognizing the danger of such a position, that at some point, some very fine but very real point, it is possible for the church to cease to be the church, and that at that point it should identify itself by some other name.

During World War II, because of the extreme shortage of coffee in Europe, authorities began putting small amounts of parched barley in the brew. Since no one could tell the difference, the amount was gradually increased. Eventually the people were drinking nothing but parched barley. But the change had come so gradually that many thought they were drinking the finest coffee.

There are two remarkable things about this story. The first is that so few people knew the difference. The second is that those who were responsible for it and who did know the difference insisted that this was indeed coffee their people were drinking and that it was a superior coffee to that of other countries. It did not contain caffeine, the aroma was more pleasant, it was easier on the digestive system.

Despite the fact that these things were true and perhaps desirably so, the true lover of coffee would have to differ with this reasoning and say that the people were drinking something other than coffee. The question is: How much barley can be put into coffee and still have coffee? When should it begin to be called by some other name? Or, with respect to the question now before us: How far can the church wander from its mission and nature and still remain the church?

The Christian faith certainly can be changed at many points so as to make it conform more to my personal preferences, more palatable, more easily acceptable, more in keeping with my culture and my way of life. But the question is: Will it be a Christian church when we have finished with this adjustment to human desires, needs, prides, and prejudices?

An adherent of the free church tradition always hesitates to use the term "heresy." But what we have been saying is that racism has negated so much of the mission and nature of the church in America that there is no other name for it except that opprobrious term—heresy. It is the question that was raised for us by the parable of the "barley-coffee" that made heresy extremely serious and dangerous throughout the history of the church. It is not that the heretics wished to oppose the true faith. On the contrary, they argued that they alone held the true faith.

The task of the church would be considerably less arduous and difficult if the racist would denounce the church. He seldom does this. Far more often he will claim to be defending the faith when he expounds his racial theories. He may denounce the clergy, or certain boards or bishops, but always the racist insists that the Christian faith does not really mean what that clergy or that board or that bishop says it means. It is the bishop, the minister, or the priest who is apostate. The racist is orthodox. It is he who loves the church and must protect it from those who preach false doctrines and would deceive the people.

Here the failure of the church today becomes patent—not because the church today spawns heresy. That has always been so. There is no reason to believe that Christian doctrine will ever be free of misunderstanding and willful distortion. The contemporary church has failed because it has not learned how to prevent racism from poisoning its life and mission. When one, within the church and in the church's name, justifies and presents a wholly un-Biblical doctrine of creation, redemption, and life in the Spirit, founded on racist presuppositions and prejudices, he is living in serious heresy; and the church, if it is to save its own life, must somehow learn to deal with him. In so doing, it does not tremble for its physical, institutional life; but it remembers that it has not been called to great numbers or great wealth, but to wholeness and health.

Chapter II

The Nature of the Problem

THE TERM "SEGREGATIONIST" MEANS MANY THINGS. It means the Ku Klux Klan and a large part of the White Citizens' Councils who support the strict separation of racial groups without reference to any other values.

It means the session member who says he would not object to having his children attend Sunday school with members of another race or living in an integrated neighborhood, but will not allow it because he fears it will lead to intermarriage.

It means the rapidly increasing Black Muslim movement among urban Negroes. This movement, whose membership lists are estimated to contain between 100,000 and 250,000 persons, advocates violence similar to that of the Klan. Unlike the "Uncle Toms" among Negroes who favored segregation because they derived some personal benefit from it, the Black Muslims oppose integration on the grounds that the white man is inferior and unfit for full citizenship in the coming black society. Not integration, but separation and the founding of a black nation on American soil, is their cry. Theirs is the voice of the disillusioned Negro masses.

The term "segregationist" means the Montgomery woman who held her small child in her arms during a mob attack on bus riders, and clung to the hair of a

Negro girl in an effort to pull her close enough for the lad to strike her in the face with his little fists.

It means the Governor of Alabama whose repeated vitriolic outbursts inflamed the passions of the mob and by innuendo invited violence. It means state legislators who use every conceivable device to evade the law of the land. It means the gentle dowager, or, as reported by the Attorney General of California, "little old ladies in tennis shoes" who dearly love their maids, their cooks, and their cocker spaniels, but believe that the term "civil rights" is a communist slogan.

"Segregationist" means restricted neighborhoods in Westchester County, New York, or hooded night riders in Mississippi. It is the Tennessee Society for the Maintenance of Segregation or the New England congregation that generously builds a mission for the colored people because "they will be happier with their own people."

The truth is that "segregationist" means most of us in one form or to one degree. It does not mean only the rabid and lunatic fringe that expends all of its energy in race hatred. For the Christian, it must also mean anyone who regards people "from a human point of view," and who classifies and categorizes members within the body of Christ.

Anyone who believes that discrimination and prejudice are peculiar to the southern region of America has only to look at the list of hate groups that have been active over the past decade. Although most of the new organizations that have sprung up since the Supreme Court's 1954 decision are located in the South, older and more established groups with headquarters in other regions have published the major portion of hate literature in this country.

Such organizations as the Christian Nationalist Crusade, headed by Gerald L. K. Smith, of Los Angeles, the American Nationalists of Inglewood, California, and the group that publishes *Common Sense* in Union, New Jersey, have blanketed areas of unrest. They have served as catalysts of violence in community after community, North and South.

Notwithstanding the fact that anti-Semitism has been the chief stock in trade of these organizations, they have more recently adopted the racial crisis as the chief vehicle by which to peddle their wares of suspicion and rancor. This has served more to stir anti-Negro feeling in the North than it has to arouse anti-Semitism in the South. Generally speaking, a dormant form of racial prejudice is more prevalent in the North than is religious bigotry (especially anti-Semitism) in the South.

While the Southern resistance groups have far more respectability than their Northern counterparts, both couch their purposes in lofty, culturally approved, and generalized terms. For example, the White Citizens' Council of Mississippi has as its slogan: "Dedicated to the maintenance of peace, good order, and domestic tranquillity in our communities and in our state and to the preservation of our state's rights."

Such high-sounding phrases create an aura of respectability about the movement and permit the central organization to be free of responsibility for the often drastic pronouncements and actions of local units. However, the organizations themselves make no attempt to conceal their belief in white supremacy, biologically, socially, ethically, and politically. They are categorically opposed to desegregation in schools, churches, and public accommodations, and frequently object to Negroes' registering and voting. The political strength of these groups is impressive. At the beginning, most of them disclaimed any political ambitions. This is no longer the case. Such groups now have virtually absolute power in one state in the South and are a significant political factor in several others. It is evident that they are not concerned only with race. In 1955, W. J. Simmons, executive secretary of the Mississippi Citizens' Council, had this to say:

I think . . . [the White Citizens' Council] is much more than a white supremacist group, and I think it is much more than a protectionist group. I think it is fundamentally the first real stirrings of a conservative revolt in this country, judging by the responses we've gotten from other states. . . . Some of the people who are attracted to this movement may not be concerned about the Negro.

Developments since Simmons' statement was voiced have proved his observation to be an accurate appraisal of the situation. Many politically conservative and reactionary organizations, among them the John Birch Society, have become working allies with the White Citizens' Councils. While the councils are most concerned with the preservation of segregation, they will gladly co-operate with other groups whose diverse aims may be, for example, to abolish the income tax or prevent the fluoridation of water. Put them all together, and in some sections of the country and on some issues you have a powerful political movement.

What does all this have to do with the renewal of the church? A great deal. First of all because these groups have succeeded in creating the image of a holy crusade. Some of them deliberately and with astute calculation see the churches as a convenient "front" for their activities. For example, Robert B. Patterson, secretary of the Citizens' Councils of America, told a group in New Orleans that they should infiltrate the churches and there take the offensive against "the mixing of the races."

"By organizing within churches," said Patterson, "foes of integration could bring pressure on ministers to support segregation and change the position of state and national church organizations which have endorsed mixing of races." He added with solemnity: "We love our churches just like we love our schools, and we want to preserve them." Protestant Patterson's advice seems to have been followed by a number of well-known Roman Catholics, and it appears that it was this kind of "creeping Protestantism" that disturbed the Archbishop to the point of exercising the seldom used but powerful weapon of excommunication.

But while the ultimate allegiance of spokesmen such as Patterson is to racial hate and while their manipulation of the churches is coldly calculated, by far the greatest number of these people are convinced that their cause is just and righteous. They are convinced that God is on their side. In seeking to maintain segregation they are doing nothing less than his will. Indeed, one of the greatest dangers we face is that the racial doctrine of white supremacy which has always been an element of secular culture in America will become a part of the church's body of dogma, an unwritten article of faith.

Perhaps the following story will illustrate how this gloomy prospect can actually be realized. One of my earliest recollections is of sitting one evening in a rural church in a Deep South county and watching the Ku Klux Klan file solemnly into the little frame building. In the ceremony that followed, a large pulpit Bible was presented by the Klansmen to the congregation and was accepted by the revival preacher. On the back cover of the book was stamped in brazen letters: K.K.K.

Several years ago I was preaching in that same pulpit and as I held the back cover of the Bible while reading the Scripture, my fingers moved across those large, embossed letters. Later in the afternoon, talking with several members of the congregation, I asked them what they thought about having a pulpit Bible in their church that had been given by the Klan and bore its symbol. Although these were people who had lived their entire lives in that community and who had been present at that original

Klan ceremony, each one stated that he had quite forgotten the incident and had never known that the letters K.K.K. were raised on the back cover of the Bible on their pulpit.

The greatest test and danger facing the Christian church in America is not racism as such, but that racism has become, consciously or unconsciously, a part of the faith. The Klan no longer exists in that rural community, but it has left its stamp not only on the cover of the Bible but on the minds and hearts of the present generation and those yet unborn. The groups which now have the prestige and power that formerly was the Klan's— the White Citizens' Councils and the John Birch Society —will also pass away. But the seedlings they are planting today will grow and thrive for a long, long time. And these seedlings are essentially religious in character. Most of what is written and distributed by groups seeking to subvert the law of church and nation has a basically religious theme. Religious meaning is increasingly being written into the race literature of the hate groups and no subject arouses more religious support in America today than the subject of race. The segregationists in pew and pulpit who appeal to such authority are not simply resorting to rationalization. The stamp of racism has become a part of their religious heritage, and for them the integrationists are those who are apostate. In the eyes of the segregationist, the man who believes in racial justice denies the faith. The true defender of Christianity is he who would keep the races forever separate in the church and in the society.

As indicated earlier, the task of the churches would be less difficult if the segregationist would say: "I like segregation in my church and neighborhood and school, and I am going to keep it that way no matter what Christ or the Bible or the church say to the contrary." If that were the situation we faced, the churches could simply put their numerous mission boards and departments of evangelism to work converting the heathen. But instead, the segregationist defends white supremacy in God's name. With Bible in his hand, and chapter and verse on his lips, he presents and documents his arguments. In the name of God he denies the love, mercy, justice, and judgment of God, and it is virtually impossible to break through and reach him.

The attempt must be made, however, and sometimes it is effectively accomplished on the level of Scripture. One of the Biblical passages most often quoted by the racists is the Genesis story of creation. (Indeed, a critic once remarked, somewhat unjustly, of a Nashville segregationist minister: "His trouble is that he never got any farther in the Bible than Genesis.") Let us now examine that well-known but much misused account of Creation.

"The blue birds and the red birds don't fly together," say the segregationists. It's true. They don't. And the Genesis account tells why:

"And God said, 'Let the earth put forth vegetation, plants yielding seed, and fruit trees bearing fruit . . . *each according to its kind.*' . . . And it was so. The earth brought forth vegetation, plants yielding seed *according to their own kinds,* and trees bearing fruit in which is their seed, *each according to its kind.* . . . God created the great sea monsters and every living creature that moves . . . *according to their kinds,* and every winged bird *according to its kind.* . . .

"And God said, 'Let the earth bring forth living creatures *according to their kinds:* cattle and creeping things and beasts of the earth *according to their kinds.*' And it was so. And God made the beasts of the earth *according to their kinds* and the cattle *according to their kinds,* and everything that creeps upon the ground *according to its kind.*" (Gen. 1:11–12, 21, 24–25; italics added.)

". . . Each according to its kind." This is probably the most important passage of Scripture in any treatment of race. The phrase, or a slight variation of it, appears no fewer than ten times in this account. But suddenly a dramatic change takes place: "Then God said, *'Let us make man in our image after our likeness'* " (Gen. 1:26, italics added).

All the other creatures had been made "each according to its kind," but man was made in the image and likeness of God! Thus man became the highest of God's creatures—not some men, by *man!* But there is still another significant note in this story. God made man in his own image. Certainly that alone makes man of considerable importance. But he also made him out of dirt! Man is at once made after the image of God and created out of that lowly commodity—dirt!

Various doctrines have sprung from these two facets of the Creation story. Some have emphasized the idea of man being a little lower than the angels and in the image of God and have insisted that he is therefore the very heart and center of the universe. Others have insisted that being made from dirt, man is precisely that—dirt, with all the connotation which that humble substance brings to mind. At this point it is not important which is the correct emphasis or interpretation. What is important is that whatever is true of a man, he is God's creature and he is one and inseparable from every other human creature.

The account of Creation, of course, does not really have to do with race. It has to do with grace; with what we could not do for ourselves because we were not. It is something unearned, undeserved, something we could not even ask for, because we were without existence and without power until God performed his creative act. For the segregationist to question creation is to question God's grace, for creation *is* grace—nothing less nor more. "It is he that made us and we are his. (Ps. 100:3.) And whether we are a little lower than the angels or as lowly as dirt, God made us, and neither the color of the angels above us nor the color of the dirt beneath our feet is important.

Interestingly enough, if the color of the dirt of which we are made is important, it really adds credence to the Black Muslim argument for black supremacy. For so-called white man isn't white at all but is about the color of hill clay, and anyone who has ever been a farmer knows hill clay won't grow much of anything except crowder peas and pine trees, while dark soil is always at a premium! But whatever we men are made of, one thing is certain—we are all of the same stuff. All of us are in the same boat and the boat is captained, not by our-selves, but by God. It is the captain above who has the right to rank and place the passengers, and God has given no indication that this is done on the basis of race.

The church must be concerned with the segregationist not only because he is within the institution, but espe-cially and above all because he too is a child of God. He too is a brother. The church cannot force the racist out of its fellowship by any arbitrary or highhanded disci-pline. The church must understand him, but at the same time it must not permit understanding him to mean that its own policy becomes silence or inaction. There is no one in America more troubled, more distressed, than the pastor who truly understands, who looks out over his congregation and his city and understands that his people are, at least in part, victims of the bitter crop of the seeds of time and the inexplicable forces of modernity which they did not plant, whose furrows they did not cultivate, but whose harvest is imposed upon them. At the same time such a pastor will know that he has no choice but to preach the uncompromising and scandaliz-ing imperatives of the gospel. Jesus understood the real condition of the people of Jerusalem, but the knowledge that certain social and political factors played a role in the popular customs and ethos of the city did not keep him from entering Jerusalem and turning it upside down.

The racist is the greatest challenge the church faces today in both the North and the South. One might say that he is the true adolescent of adult Christianity; the most unlovely and the most in need of love. Certainly the church must not tolerate what he stands for, but it must not abandon him in its attempt to force him to maturity. Those of us who consider ourselves the children of light with respect to our attitudes and practices in race relations must ask ourselves what happened in our lives to make us so different from the racist. What combination of genes, what freak of historical circumstance and personal association, gave us vision to see the truth? Even if God laid his hands on us, even if some are chosen, to what credit can we claim, what reason have we to boast, and what right to condemn? Somehow we cannot hate the racist, for most of us do not know how or when we left his ranks, if we have left them at all.

I have seen and known the resentment of the racist, his hostility, his frustration, his need for someone upon whom to lay blame and to punish. I know he is mistaken, misguided, and willfully disobedient, but somehow I am not able to distinguish between him and myself. My sins may not be his, but they are no less real and no less heinous. Perhaps I have been too close to this man. Perhaps if I had not heard his anguished cry when the rains didn't come in time to save his cotton, if I had not felt the severity of his economic deprivation, if I had not looked upon his agony on Christmas Eve while I, his six-year-old child, feigning sleep, waited for a Santa who would never come; if I had not been one of him through these gales of tragedy, I would be able to condemn him without hesitation. If I had not shared his plight; if I had not lived with him in an atmosphere of suspicion, distrust, ignorance, misinformation, and nefarious political leadership, surely my heart would break less when I see him fomenting mob violence in front of *his* schoolhouse and *his* church house. Perhaps I would not pity him as much if I were not from his loins. But pity him I do.

But the church must not pity the racist. It must love and redeem him. It must somehow set him free. With the same love that it is commanded to shower upon the innocent victim of his frustration and hostility, the church must love the racist. Moreover, the church is called to love those who use and exploit both the racists and their victims for personal wealth and political gain. The church must stand in love and judgment upon the victim, the victimized, and those, both black and white, who exploit both, for they are all the children of God.

Chapter III

The Gods of Law and Order

PRIOR TO 1954, MOST OF THE PROTESTANT DENOMI-
nations in the United States were relatively silent on the
question of race. Since that year innumerable statements,
resolutions, and pronouncements on segregation and discrimination have come from virtually all the major Protestant groups. Many of them begin by endorsing the
Supreme Court decision of May 17, 1954, on segregation
in public education. Most of them call for harmonious
relations and a calm acceptance of what the court has
decreed. Almost all deplore violence, but few choose to
vex themselves with the thought of what their position
would be if the court's decision and Christian doctrine
were not in agreement. Indeed, it would almost appear
that the court had made a decision binding upon Christians that the churches had no competence to make for
themselves.

Before 1954, most liberal churches and churchmen
were not insistent upon a doctrinaire position of strict
obedience to the law. Today the American churches argue
that segregation must be abolished because it is illegal.
It is interesting to note, however, that for some years, at
least a few churches and churchmen occasionally admonished their people to join in disobedience to law if
such law was patently contrary to the will of God.

26

For example, delivering the Knapp Lecture at the University of Wisconsin on March 19, 1952, Chancellor Harvie B. Branscomb, of Vanderbilt University, said:

The second contribution which religion has made to American life has been the insistence upon a law of God which is supreme above all human institutions and man-made legislation. To this divine law man owes final obedience. If the laws of state or government deviate from this standard, they have no moral authority and, in fact, should be disregarded or rejected. ("The Contribution of Moral and Spiritual Ideas to the Making of The American Way of Life," p. 11.)

Eight years later, one of Chancellor Branscomb's students, the Rev. James M. Lawson, Jr., had this to say about the breaking of law:

Defiant violation of the law is a contradiction of my entire understanding of and loyalty to Christian nonviolence. When the Christian considers the concept of civil disobedience as an aspect of nonviolence, it is only within the context of a law or a law enforcement agency which has in reality ceased to be the law, and then the Christian does so only in fear and trembling before God. (*Nashville Banner,* March 3, 1960.)

Even a cursory glance at these two statements will show that Chancellor Branscomb's words are considerably more emphatic and uncompromising than those of the student. Yet Mr. Lawson was expelled from Vanderbilt by the chancellor on the allegation that he "advocated a planned campaign of civil disobedience."

There is no evidence to suggest that Chancellor Branscomb was insincere either in 1952 or in 1960. It seems more likely that the events of the past eight years brought a change in his position. Dr. Branscomb has never favored racial segregation in his public policies and has worked diligently to effect desegregation on his own campus. Prior to 1954 he had insisted that if the laws of the state were in conflict with the laws of God, the laws of the state should be disregarded or rejected. In fact, he did disregard them when he desegregated Vanderbilt University, for the law of Tennessee holds that private schools may not have Negroes and whites in the same classrooms. As late as 1960 he was still speaking in behalf of racial justice, but now he maintained that this must be accomplished within the framework of man-made, not God-ordained, legislation.

There seems to have been a similar change in the position of many of the churches. The churches with dispatch adopted the dictum that the clear duty of the Christian is always to obey the law when, in 1954, the law became what the churches wanted it to be. Advising their people to desegregate because the law said to do so seemed less risky than taking a bold position based on the Christian doctrine of man, the Biblical imperative of justice, and the doctrine of the sovereignty of God.

But the worship of law proved quickly to be a two-edged sword. For the integrationist Christian it was pleasant to be able to say, "The law is on our side!" But the segregationist Christian was able to argue on the same basis. Particularly in the South, he had clear and unequivocal legislation at the state and local levels which explicitly forbade any form of racial mixing. He could argue convincingly that there is nothing in the Christian body of doctrine which holds that federal laws are any more sacred than state or local laws.

The legal argument within the churches made for further confusion when those favoring desegregation began arguing for disobedience to law in the sit-in movement during 1959–1960. The General Assembly of The United Presbyterian Church in the U.S.A., meeting in May, 1960, went on record as advocating a degree of civil disobedience when it said among other things: "Affirming that some laws and customs requiring racial discrimination are, in our judgment, such serious violations of the law of God as to justify peaceable and orderly disobedience or disregard of these laws . . ." The National Council of the Protestant Episcopal Church and several other groups took similar positions. One could assume that this was a swing away from the "let us obey the law" position which developed immediately following the Supreme Court decision of 1954 and a stronger ground upon which to fight. But one week after the United Presbyterian General Assembly took its action in Cleveland, a spokesman for the White Citizens' Council in New Orleans strongly recommended and called for a campaign of civil disobedience (as a matter of conscience) to combat desegregation of the New Orleans public schools! On the other hand, in Montgomery, Alabama, when Negro demonstrators were rudely handled by state and city police and a group of citizens who had been quickly deputized as a mounted force to assist in the brutal dispersion of the demonstrators, the local ministerial alliance had the following to say:

Let us continue to depend upon law and order administered with a concern for all citizens to stabilize our society.

The appeal to law is at best a confused picture within the churches. We must say quite frankly that it appears that the churches have often used it to evade their deeper responsibility. It has been the easy way. But the church has not always appealed to law for the rightness of its action. Here is another kind of statement regarding this problem:

We believe it is sinful to have two congregations in the same community for persons of separate and distinct races. That race prejudice would cause trouble in the churches we know. It did this in apostolic days. Not once did the apostles suggest that they should form separate congregations for the different races. But they always admonished them to unity, forbearance, love, and brotherhood in Christ Jesus.

Upon first glance this would appear to be just another statement among the reams of resolutions and pronouncements that have heated the presses for the past seven years. And it would surely be assumed that such a statement represents the view of the more liberal church bodies, for it moves far beyond schools, parks, and lunch counters; and it affirms without equivocation that if there are two congregations in one town because of race, one of them should be abandoned. Actually the statement comes from one of the most conservative groups in Protestantism. The man who wrote it was far from notorious for his social liberalism. He was David Lipscomb, a Church of Christ evangelist. He made the statement in an article on "Race Prejudice," in the February, 1878, issue of *Gospel Advocate,* when a Texas Church of Christ congregation objected to a Negro who sought to affiliate with the local church. David Lipscomb was one of the foremost leaders of that denomination, and one of its colleges (still segregated) bears his name today.

Lipscomb's statement is important for several reasons. In the first place it is generally thought that we have come a long way in race relations since 1878 and that if given time, patience, and understanding we will "work this thing out" in our churches. Yet in 1878 a spokesman for the most conservative group called it a sin to have separate congregations because of race, while almost a hundred years later in the most liberal groups we still have, not only racial congregations, but racial synods in the Presbyterian Church, the Central Jurisdiction for Negroes in the Methodist, separate judicatories in almost every communion, and a racial ministry in all.

But an even more remarkable feature of this statement, in the light of which we might re-examine our own positions, is that it made no appeal to harmony *or* to the law. Many church appeals and pronouncements today are based on one or the other of these prime values. Lipscomb's was not. With respect to harmony within the fellowship, he did not try to avoid conflict but seemed to think that harmony or its absence was irrelevant to the question at hand. In an almost casual manner he moved on to state what was for him the heart of the matter. Apparently to this spokesman of a group sometimes referred to as a "fringe sect," the problem of Christian behavior had nothing to do with what people *wanted* to do, or were *ready* to do, or with what did or did not violate the local mores. Like many before his time and since, Lipscomb recognized the test that the church faced by its double concern for conformity and loyalty to God. Implicit in his statement was what social scientists have indicated in our own time: there is a difference between prejudice and discrimination, between feeling and behavior. In effect, Lipscomb said: Surely there is such a thing as race prejudice in all of us who are in the churches, and it will cause trouble. So what? His was the strange notion that Christian behavior had to do only with the uncompromising demands of Almighty God as revealed through the life and teachings of Jesus Christ.

Contrast this to our day when cardinal virtues are harmony within the fellowship, peace, good will, "tact" on the part of the preacher, dignity and respectability of approach, law and order, constitutions, status, preservation of public schools and property values. All these values are important to us and doubtless were to the group for whom Mr. Lipscomb spoke, but they did not seem primary. Lipscomb made no appeal to law, to the courts, to democracy, or to any political ideology. His was a simple proclamation: "Thus saith the Lord." This despite the fact that the Emancipation Proclamation and the tumult of Reconstruction were as close to him and fully as controversial as recent Supreme Court decisions on civil rights are to us.

If arguments for law and order, peace and harmony,

are irrelevant to the church's concern on race, so are appeals to the social sciences and humanitarianism. These are all valuable and valid approaches, but they are not the distinctive approaches of the church. Law and order is the business of government, social science is the concern of the sociologists and anthropologists, and humanitarianism is the inspiration of thousands of dedicated men and women who spend their lives alleviating human suffering. All of these have a place in the church; and the church, which has learned much from these sources, cannot ignore them. But the church must not be distracted by them. Its concern is more profound and more radical than any of these.

The advocate of racial justice often loses the argument because he permits his antagonist to choose the weapon and field of battle. The racist usually meets us on sociological grounds, and we become social scientists because it is so simple to refute his arguments one by one, and we are deluded into believing that thereby we have won the day. He says the minority group is dirt, is low in intelligence and lax in morals, is less ambitious, doesn't pay his just share of the taxes, is shiftless, lazy, and uncouth. Such arguments are easy to answer on sociological grounds. We can explain to him that he really means achievement and not intelligence, and we can point out why this is true. It is no difficult matter to show that morality is a relative matter. The double standard and the success of the majority group in keeping its questionable morals under wraps will document the case. We can say that a group which is the last to be hired and the first to be fired would understandably have less ambition, for what is the use of trying under such circumstances? We can say that taxes are paid on income, and if we give the minority jobs with higher income, they would then pay more taxes. We can skillfully puncture the racist's stereotypes one by one. But generally he remains unconvinced.

The real question takes us in another direction. Why should we rely upon our knowledge of the social sciences when there is a Christian answer? If we use *that* answer, if *we* pick the field of battle, the segregationist has less advantage. The Christian answer is that whether or not his analysis is correct, God has not called us into the body of Christ, into the fellowship of the redeemed, the church, because we are clean or have superior intelligence or high morals. He has called us into a fellowship in which we are all unclean, lazy, uncouth, lax in morality, low in ambition; in which we are all undeserving yet loved and accepted of God, our common Father. In our present state of sophistication in the churches we might find it difficult to give this answer, but it is nearer the truth than the attempt to refute racial stereotypes. Race is not a rational matter. The consciousness of race, ethnocentrism, as even some social scientists admit, is largely a state of mind and it is difficult to combat a state of mind by logical refutation. God made no such approach when he brought man into being and when he stooped to save him. His move was irrational, foolishness, a stumbling block. A king was born amidst sheep manure and murdered as an enemy of the people and a subverter of the state. What possible rational argument can we devise from the story of Creation and redemption. And yet this is all we have to offer. This is the distinctive Christian apologia.

Why should we not grant the segregationist his facts? They are not always accurate. But what if they are? Let others boast of *facts!* Ours is a faith that transcends facts to lay hold upon truth. Our task is not to refute by facts, but to lead the racist to see that when he confronts the Christ he claims to serve, his facts are irrelevant.

From a rational point of view, the segregationist sometimes has sound arguments. And the churches themselves have sometimes used the same arguments. In several places, for example, the churches have established schools when public facilities have been closed. History has already recorded the fact that, when the secular culture failed to preserve segregation, the churches took up the fight and held on for yet a little while. Why did we do it? We did it for the sake of good, for the advancement of knowledge, for the increase of wisdom, for the sake of our children. No one will question these motives. It cannot be denied that we have a responsibility to our children. Who would be prepared to argue that Christians ought to suffer their children, black or white, to grow up in ignorance?

These are rational values. They appeal to the common sense of ordinary men and women. But what is their real validity within the fellowship of believers? In the final analysis, when our most rational arguments and common sense appeals fail to fill the yawning void of unfaith, when we stand nakedly under the command of God, we know that these values we have worshiped are creatures of the false gods of race and culture.

A young white Christian mother once said to me in Little Rock that she could never again send her child to one of the schools established to evade the law as long as they accept her child but refuse the child of another mother because of some degree of skin pigmentation. She could not permit herself this privilege, she said, and maintain her integrity as a member of a church which in its public posture stood for equality and brotherhood. She reported with some emotion how it felt deliberately to sacrifice her son when by one stroke of the pen she could save him. She was in good company.

"Take your son, your only son Isaac, . . . and go to the land of Moriah, and offer him there as a burnt offering upon one of the mountains of which I shall tell you. . . . And Abraham took the wood of the burnt offering and laid it on Isaac his son; and he took in his hand the fire and the knife. So they went both of them together.

. . . Then Abraham put forth his hand, and took the knife to slay his son." (Gen. 22:2, 6, 10.)

Compared with this radical faithfulness, how puny and petty our rationalizations about our property values, our children's future, our neighborhood pride, must be to the Creator. We cannot obey the teachings of our church and our nation, we say, because it will injure our little children! Whether this prediction of the tragedy that will befall our children is true or untrue is not yet clear. It is true, by the mind and spirit of Christ, that this is not the first question we must answer. Is it even worthy of debate? This Little Rock mother (she and others like her have been the salvation of that city) was right. It was that kind of obedience that made the faith of Abraham a great religion and his righteousness imputed to the New Israel of Christ.

"He who loves son or daughter more than me is not worthy of me" (Matt. 10:37), said a man whom most racists, North and South, still call Lord. This is the question before the church in America: Do we believe in the God of Abraham, Isaac, and Jacob, the God and Father of our Lord Jesus Christ, or do we worship at the shrine of state sovereignty, restricted neighborhoods, white schools, and racial supremacy? Today it is white supremacy; there is a good chance that tomorrow it will be black supremacy. Either is contrary to the will and purpose of God, and no amount of rationalization will be able to obscure that truth.

Chapter IV

The Humanistic Detour

THE SEGREGATIONIST CHRISTIAN IS PLAYING A MOST significant role in the life of the church. He is constantly forcing those who consider themselves the children of light to defend and define the Christian message. If when we begin to define and defend what we think is the Christian message, we discover that it is little more than a sentimental veil of humanism, it is because we have not met the segregationist on the field upon which the Christion must fight. When we speak, it is most often of law and order, of human dignity, of man's rights, of democracy, of constitution, and, at best, of the principle of the brotherhood of man and the fatherhood of God. More and more this has become the most unfavorable terrain for battle. The humanist has done a great service to mankind by supporting the egalitarian line. But for the Christian church to assume this role is to court failure. We fail for two reasons. First, we cannot do well what the secular and humanist organizations can do. Our churches can become adjuncts to human relations councils and civil rights organizations, but this is to sell what we have much too short. For what we have to say is far more radical, far more demanding, far more inclusive of all of society than anything the humanistically oriented groups have said. If race is not a valid concept in Christian doctrine, there is no room to debate such irrelevancies as who sits where on a bus, who lives in which neighborhood, and who marries whom on the basis of propriety, law and order, and egalitarian philosophy.

As we have championed the humanistic arguments, we have also tended to become more and more humanitarian in our action programing. When a church organization needs personnel in the field of human relations it is inclined to look for effective, skilled social reformers or human engineers, but rarely preachers and prophets. There is a considerable difference. Doubtless the church historically has made use of both, and will continue to do so; but in our effort to find renewal for the church in the area of race relations, it is necessary to say more than that all men are brothers and ought to act brotherly. For we know that all men are not going to act like brothers and that the Christian faith has a great deal to say beyond that point. Moreover, our critics raise valid questions as to whether or not the church has any concern or right to be concerned with the desegregation of society so long as its own record is so dismal. If all church institutions, colleges and universities, hospitals, medical schools, secondary and primary schools, camps, assembly grounds, congregations, homes for aged and orphanages were open to all, there would not be very much remaining for society to do.

It is often said that we have this concern for justice as citizens of our nation; that as Christian citizens we must exercise this responsibility within structures of law and order which also have their influence upon the church. There is truth here. Action in society has often influenced the pattern of church life. But are we not also, and foremost, citizens of the Kingdom of God? What right have I to indict a real estate agent for restricting residential developments when my own church will not admit anyone other than white Protestants to its home for the retired? The admonition, "Physician, heal yourself" (Luke 4:23), is appropriate. To ignore it or even to offer rebuttal to what it implies is to add to our already abundant hypocrisy.

The second and more important reason we fail is that the Christian message on race does not depend upon egalitarian premises and arguments. Ours is not a message of law and order, of man's rights, of constitutions. The Christian view of race is not limited to the principle of the fatherhood of God and the brotherhood of man. When we tell the segregationist that the gospel is to obey the law and accept the Supreme Court decision, he can see no gospel, no "good news" here. This, for him, is only bad news, and he is not wrong to ridicule the church and tell it to mind its own business.

Of course, the segregationist is wrong if he means that the church should steer clear of controversy, but he is right when he says that purely humanistic values are not our basic concern. He is likewise right when he insists that the gospel is not a proclamation of what we ought to do.

But if he is told, as he *must* be told, that the Christian gospel was and is a message of grace and redemption, then it is an entirely different matter. Tell the segregationist that by this grace God became flesh—flesh meaning "like one of us." Tell him God was in this flesh. Tell him the *Christian* message on race relations and all human relations: God was in Christ reconciling the world to himself. God was in Christ reconciling his children to one another and thus to himself. God was in Christ breaking down the walls of hostility that separate man from man and all men from God. God, furthermore, was in Christ loving him—the segregationist himself; loving him, accepting him, forgiving him, even if he cannot yet love and accept and forgive his brother. This is what we have to say to the segregationist, whether he belongs to a Black Nationalist movement in Harlem, a White Property Owners' Association in Chicago, or a Citizens' Council in Birmingham. If he hears this and accepts it, there is more likelihood of achieving an integrated church in an integrated society than if we simply tell him that he should go home and be good, or that he ought to obey the law.

Those who take the position that there is no specific program of Christian race relations—that we must take our cue from economics, politics, and sociology—are mistaken. That is simply to say that there is no Christian message. It is well that the racist forces us to hear that message anew, and in the hearing will be our true renewal. The Christian message on race is nothing more nor less than the Christian message. It has to do with grace, not law, not order. That something has been done for us, something free, something with which we had nothing to do, something undeserved and unearned. It is the mercy and grace of God which has given us newness of life. In this "new creation" (II Cor. 5:17), we are neither Caucasian, African, Asian, male nor female, bond nor free. We are a third race. All our human engineering is vain if we miss the unambiguous point that, in the message of grace, race is irrelevant. The only relevant point has to do with redemption, not race, class, or caste. This is not an invitation to complacency by the preacher. This is no license to mumble, "God was in Christ, let us pray." This is not pious quietism. The relevance of this grace, this creative act of God, must ever be spelled out and applied over and over again in the rough and tumble of daily life.

Of course, we are reminded that this message of grace has been preached for two thousand years and that little has changed. Preaching just does not seem to achieve for us the goal of an inclusive church and society. The world goes merrily on its segregated way, and churches go on being exclusive. Businessmen from our ranks go on discriminating in hiring, in placement, and in promotions. Inevitably we feel that we must devise gimmicks, develop techniques. We are overwhelmed by the drive to be *effective*. It is at this point that we call upon the social scientists, the human engineers, the race relations specialists. We adopt uncritically the sophisticated methods of our secular colleagues. If we tell the cultured despisers among them that "God was in Christ" (II Cor. 5:19), so that "you are all one" (Gal. 3:28), they are apt to wink slyly and chuckle. "A bunch of squares." Unrealistic, utopian. And so we compete with each other in the "do it yourself" market of the latest methods, techniques, and gimmicks. What we seem to have difficulty remembering is that we *are* a bunch of squares—we Christians.

The message we have is not the "latest word" or the most intellectually respectable; it is the same scandal, the same stumbling block it has always been. It does not reject method or spurn success, but it does not depend upon either for its ultimate validity. Our task is not to be successful—as if success proved validity. Our task is to proclaim the gospel. Proclamation means more than verbalizing from the pulpit, to be sure, and yet we can find no substitute for the sacrament of the Word. The world may not hear us. It never really has. But the message has not lost its power, and when it seems not to be heard, not to be *effective,* that is the time to proclaim it with greater resolve.

Crash programs and grand strategies may make us more acceptable to the public, the press, and the secular agencies in the field of race relations; but our "crash program" was initiated and has been accomplished; our "grand strategy" was designed and fulfilled centuries ago. And indeed not in a court of law, not within a political document, but in a tragic scene of bloody sweat and agonizing death on a scarred hillside outside the city of Jerusalem. If the world cannot see the error and folly of racism, if it cannot see that racial consciousness and prejudice is in conflict with the program and strategy of redemption, if it does not repent of the dreadful sin of racial exclusiveness as a result of our practice and proclamation of the gospel, then God has judged us and we are his impotent people. But, if as his servants we will not preach the gospel and will not demonstrate in our own ranks the oneness of all men as creatures of God, we will have sat in judgment upon God, and there will be nothing but frustration and failure for such a church. When that day comes, and God forbid that it has already arrived, we will have long since ceased to be the people of God.

The oneness of all men to which we are alluding does not have to do with man. It is possible that we are ineffective in race relations because we begin at the wrong place—with both the wrong subject and the wrong object. Churches frequently begin their Christian social concern programing by pointing out the suffering and deprivation of the minority group—photographs of undernourished children without shoes, standing outside of tar-paper shacks or in slum ghettos, their brown faces reflecting the confusion and sadness of heart of those who have too soon come to understand that the world holds for them few of its privileges. Anyone who cannot empathize with these victims of a ruthless and selfish society is far gone. Yet is there anything peculiarly Christian about such empathy? Does this express the authentic response of the church?

As one who has spent the last five years trying to minister in the numerous racial crises of the South, I know how easy it is to be motivated by feelings of pity and sympathy. Watching a mother stumble feebly along behind the casket of her son, murdered by a mob; going with a pastor into what is left of his church after a sack of dynamite has been thrown into it in the dark of Christmas Eve; seeing the bewilderment and pain of children whose presents, carefully concealed by Santa, are now broken and scattered throughout the debris of the manse; seeing a mother struck with a bottle as she takes her little girl to school; watching a pastor kicked and spat upon as he walks holding the trusting little hand of a six-year-old parishioner who is not yet old enough to be told that the screaming, unruly mob is there because she is going inside, that seven hundred grown men and women are terrified and frightened of her, one little six-year-old child—these are scenes which tear out the heart. Christian concern to correct such injustices as these is not just effusive sentimentality.

But the reactions that such scenes stir within us are not necessarily Christian reactions. At any rate this is not where we begin. To do so is surely to confuse subject and object; to be falsely oriented for Christian action. This is the starting point of the humanist. Certainly we must admit that from this point he has borne a most creditable witness. But the concern of the Christian is more basic. It is at least a different concern.

The Christian must first of all be concerned with souls. He will leap to the side of those who are being harmed, but his anguish at the suffering of the victims of racism will not blind him to the dangers facing the souls of the oppressors. The suffering of the minority group does not separate it from God, but the sin of the majority group *does* separate it from God. Thus, the soul of the dispossessor must concern us as much as the suffering of the dispossessed, and when this is not the case, our concern and action is something less than Christian concern and action. Even in terms of strategy, one-sided emphasis on the suffering is not very effective. For the suffering of the minority group does not greatly impress the dispossessor. He has grown callous to it and does not really see, much less is he shamed, by the tar-paper shack, the bare feet, the exclusion from jobs, the residential restrictions. For him, it has always been this way. These are realities of the normal white world in which he lives. He is surprised and angered that anyone would suppose that they should be otherwise. Let me illustrate.

In Fayette County, Tennessee, Negro farmers have been evicted from the land because they dared register to vote. A blacklist was circulated throughout the county through a long cold winter, with the naked ground for a floor. One man was shot with a high-powered rifle while asleep in his tent. His wife and children fled in terror into the darkness of a December night. Crop loans were denied tenant farmers even when a Federal court enjoined the owners from turning them off the land. A baby was born in one of the shabby, mud-splattered tents. An elderly woman had pneumonia. Local doctors reportedly denied medical aid to any Negro person who had registered to vote. A blacklist was circulated throughout the country with names of those who had registered, as a convenience for merchants who agreed to refuse to sell them groceries and supplies.

These conditions stimulated a rash of material aid from denominational groups throughout the country. One church agency sent volunteers to put floors in the tents. Others provided money for relief. Another purchased a four-hundred acre farm and relocated several families from the tents. This was action that should have been taken, and it was taken with the purest motivation. No one could deny the responsibility of the churches to provide assistance to people without clothing, shelter, and food. Yet we failed to minister to the majority group, the dispossessors. There is some question, therefore, whether the whole gospel of redemption was heard and heeded by the people of Fayette County.

This pattern is repeated in virtually every case. And consequently the segregationist has been able to see a major weakness in our social action. He has seen our marked similarity to the purely secular and humanistic groups. He has seen that we have generally made the deprived the subject and him the object. In terms of simple strategy—a word that requires reinterpretation in the Christian vocabulary—the dispossessors might well have been more influenced, and the injustices corrected more quickly, if *they* had been the subject of church concern; if, at the same time, there had been a ministry to them. If the segregationist had been told that what was happening to the suffering and the disinherited was not as dangerous as what was happening to him, he might have listened. If he had been warned that the judgment of God was upon him, not upon the victims, that *he* was separated from God because of his deeds, such a witness would, at least, have had strategic significance in terms of the church's objectives.

None of this is to deny the obligation of the Christian to relieve the suffering of the oppressed. It is rather to say that when this is all we do, we are stopping short of the Christian imperative. Jesus showed concern and pain when he saw people suffer, and he relieved them. But in a moment of great emotion, he looked out over his own people and cried: "O Jerusalem, Jerusalem, killing the prophets, and stoning those who are sent to you! How often would I have gathered your children together as a hen gathers her brood under her wings, and you would not!" (Matt. 23:37). Here was real tragedy. This was not merely sympathy for the suffering of the prophets. This was a cry of despair over the alienation and sin of the people. To be sure, their hardness of heart, their stubbornness, their refusal to recognize truth, resulted in human misery, but this was not primary. The suffering was merely a symptom of a functional and basic sickness. And it was for this that he went to his death.

If there is something missing in most denominational approaches to the problem of race in America today, it is

that which the secularist rightly espies as our weakness—
feeling, emotion, a maudlin sense of tragedy. Christian
compassion is not the cheap sentimentality of the junior
choir performing "I'd Rather Have Jesus," but the white-
hot emotion and indignation of the prophets, the piercing
experience of the pathos and stark tragedy of man's condition, the brokenheartedness of the truly penitent, the
groaning of man under his burden of guilt. A woman
once explained to me how she had been indifferent about
the problem of race in her city until she became a Christian. (And the term "became a Christian" had special
meaning for this person who had been "born and reared"
in the church.) When I asked her how she behaved
differently after becoming a Christian, what difference
it had made in her behavior toward other races and
groups, her response was instant. "Only one difference," she replied. "One difference. Now my heart is
broken."

Religion still involves *feeling,* and of God it can still
be said: "The sacrifice acceptable to God is a broken
spirit; a broken and contrite heart, O God, thou wilt not
despise" (Ps. 51:17). Too much of our programing in
the field of race relations has been of the coldly objective,
human engineering variety which precludes a broken
heart. It is a bringing of the Thanksgiving baskets, the
counting of noses for the poor children's Christmas party;
the coins thrown into the special collection; programs
of manipulation; designs for maneuvering, *handling* people into the Kingdom. We talk much about reconciliation.
But too often we understand by the word something that
can be accomplished by getting people together in buzz
groups or by some other clever technique of group dy-
namics. There can be no questioning the value of providing opportunities for people to communicate. But com-
munication is no substitute for reconciliation, and there
can be no reconciliation without repentance. Nor can

there be renewal of the church without repentance. And repentance comes with suffering, with a broken spirit and a contrite heart. No other possibility is available for the Christian. None of the steps can be skipped. It is a broken heart-repentance-forgiveness-reconciliation-renewal sequence that expresses the order of salvation.

In moving toward a starting point in Christian race relations, we should not forget that grace, redemption, and judgment are words the segregationists will hear. He may not understand them in the finest orthodox sense, but the sound of them is not unfamiliar even out of the "Bible belt." For many people there is not yet in these terms the emotional block there may be for other words. If, for instance, a Southern segregationist is told that it is the United States Constitution that is supreme and he is just beginning to regard seriously his own state constitution of 1890, he may find it difficult to understand why a constitution with which he feels he had nothing to do should be more sacred than one much closer to home. If he is told that the gospel is a message of law and order, he is apt to ask, whose law and what order? Or if he is told that the Christian view on race is the universal principle of the fatherhood of God and the brotherhood of man, he can make a rather convincing case to the contrary by a quick recitation of Scripture. "But to all who received him, who believed in his name, he gave power to become children of God." (John 1:12.) But if he is told that the acute problem of race has to do with the judgment of God upon his people, that it is a symptom of man's estrangement from God and a symbol of the brokenness of the body of Christ; if he is told that we are liars when we say we are in the light but hate our brothers (I John 2:9); if he is warned that it is the last hour (I John 2:18 ff.) for the Christian and for the church, this is language he may be able to understand. This is the profound and prophetic Word of the church which is the bearer of the judgment of God that pins a man's back to the wall.

It is true that we have outgrown the scorched flesh policy of Jonathan Edwards' evangelism, but few Americans are so secularized as to have no sense of the meaning of the judgment of God upon his people. Whatever that meaning may be in New York, or Atlanta, or Biloxi, we should remember (and this is especially true in the South) that the racist is seldom an atheist. Usually, in so far as he is able, he is a godly man. The message of Christianity still suggests to him that "in Christ," he can overcome his culture and his glands—in short, his prejudice. He may not have found this to be true, but he still has an uneasy feeling that it may be true nevertheless.

The redemptive purpose of Jesus Christ and the judgment of God upon his people are more than distantly related to race relations. They are at the very heart and core of the solution. Though this is not quite the starting point, it is close. Moreover, this is not a message for the majority group alone. The disease exists just as acutely in the minority group as it does in the majority. It is no startling discovery to say that original sin is not peculiar to white people. And it would sound defensive and commonplace to say it, if those of us active in the broad field of race relations did not so often realize that we were bringing one message to the prejudiced and another to the victims of prejudice. The message is not divided. There may be differences of degree and manifestation, but the sins are the same in both groups. About this we will say more in a later chapter. At the moment it is sufficient to point out that while the church did not go to the majority group in Fayette County, Tennessee, with the Christian message of judgment and redemption, neither was this its ministry to the minority group.

Despite the fact of infighting within the protest movement, the jockeying for power and position, the brokenness here, the disharmony there, the shattered fellowship within the Negro group in some ways more serious than the relationship between the two races, the churches had nothing to say. Should we not have spoken to the sharp division within the Negro groups, to the bitterness of their lawsuits, to their litigation tying up funds and relief supplies while people were hungry, to the enjoining of one another from administering relief and claiming mail, to the factionalism which found each group breaking off and announcing to the public that it alone was legitimate and true guardian of the welfare of the people? Most of our religious agencies were aware of this situation but, for the most part, the position was taken that we could not involve ourselves in the internal affairs of the movement, but would relieve the suffering of the innocent as best we could. Certainly the suffering had to be relieved, but there were no innocent. All were guilty, all were sinners and stood in desperate need of the message of judgment and redemption. Somehow, the churches have not yet learned to be critical of the new and dramatic protest movements. But they too must hear the gospel of the Lord who burns and heals. Whenever the church has been exclusively concerned with symptoms, with obvious, surface problems, choosing wrong subjects and wrong objects, it has brought forth fallacious answers. We have asked inappropriate questions and have moved into Christian social action from the wrong point of departure and with a superficial understanding of the depth of man's involvement in sin.

Chapter V

The Christian Concern and Starting Point

WE CAN NOW BEGIN TO PROBE MORE DEEPLY INTO the reasons for the church's failure in race relations. Part of the answer has already been hinted—the preoccupation with law and order, the emphasis on humanistic arguments for desegregation, and the often uncritical reliance on sociological approaches. But an important question remains: Why has the church chosen this path? At least a partial explanation lies in the organizational structure of American Protestantism. Here sociological analysis can be useful without being permitted to define the form the church should take in its mission.

From the point of view of social effectiveness, Protestantism has had difficulty making a witness in the crisis of American race relations, partly because it has had no widely recognized spokesmen, no clearly defined lines of authority for policy and action, and no strong lay support. Generally speaking, when the Roman Catholic Church has been attacked, all three of these factors have been used to support the church and sustain its decisions. Its laity consistently rally to its defense. Societies and action groups are organized to engage in energetic campaigns of propaganda and moral support. Authoritative spokesmen make declarations of policy, and lines of implementation are cleared and effectively utilized.

When the positions of the Protestant churches or of the individual clergymen are attacked, on the other hand, frequently it is our own laymen who gather the faggots. An example is seen in the fact that in several states of the Southeast, laymen of Protestant denominations have organized to oppose actively the official position of their churches on race relations. They have organized within the churches themselves and have used church machinery to launch attacks against those very churches.

Such groups as the Methodist Laymen's League of Alabama have done much to prevent the local parishes from putting into action—or even discussing—the position of the national church. They have been successful in eliminating from the conference ministers whom they deem "undesirable," and they exert considerable influence from the local congregation to the General Conference. In other regions of the country, laymen join such organizations as the John Birch Society and actively participate in propaganda diametrically opposed to that for which their churches stand.

I am not pleading here for a monolithic ecclesiastical structure, nor for an infallible clergy. My point is simply that American pulpits do not have the authority requisite for leadership in social change. Our elected officials and professional staffs charged with the social witness of the denominations do not possess sufficient authority to represent the church in such a way as to help it become an effective influence for change in society. I am also saying that pulpits must be free or there is no hope for the churches in a crisis as filled with emotional intensity as the race issue. Unless the Word of God is heard, how will it be able to combat the pressures of culture upon the thinking of the people? "Woe to me if I do not preach the gospel! (I Cor. 9:16.) But woe to a people who will not tolerate the preaching of the gospel in their own sanctuaries. And woe to the church that will not permit its officials to implement its policies.

Two permanent elements constitute the means of grace in Protestantism. The first of these is the preaching of the Word; the second is the sacrament of Holy Communion. Both declare the gospel—equally and indispensably. It is a curious fact that, despite the gag that has been applied against preaching, it has been only rarely that a clergyman has been physically barred from God's altar to administer the holy mysteries. Yet this sacred service speaks more eloquently of the unity of all God's people, of the redemptive purpose and message of Jesus Christ, and of the sin of segregation, than do all the words that a pastor may be forbidden to speak during a long tenure.

It would be a mistake, however, to push too far the argument that the blame for the church's inadequacy lies principally in its organizational structure. If the lack of a strong hierarchy were the sole or even the chief reason for the weakness of Protestantism in race relations, we should have expected a much better record from the Roman Catholics, for that communion is not burdened with such organizational deficiencies.

In fact, however, this has not been the case. Catholicism's record in race relations, like Protestantism's, has been spotty—good in some places, poor in others. On the whole there is probably little to choose between the two. Two years after the desegregation of public schools in New Orleans, for example, the city's parochial schools are just beginning to desegregate, despite promises to the contrary from the Archbishop several years ago. In the fall of 1961, when the Atlanta public schools were desegregated with great appreciation in Washington and nationwide attention, the color bar remained in full force at the parochial schools.

In Nashville, on the other hand, the desegregation of

the parochial schools preceded that of the public schools by two years. Yet in Memphis, a city in the same diocese with a far larger Catholic population than Nashville, the parochial schools are still segregated. The fact remains, however, that where Catholicism has been most effective in this struggle, its obvious advantage has been unity and organizational structure geared for action. But there must be another, more basic reason for the church's failure, and not only for the failure of the church, both Protestant and Catholic, but for failure of American society as a whole.

In the last chapter we saw that when Christians choose the dispossessed minority as their only subject of concern they will usually meet with failure. There the emphasis was that as Christians we have a clear and unmistakable responsibility and mandate to lighten the burden of our brothers whoever they are and wherever we find them. We cannot escape our obligation to aid and console the brokenhearted, whenever God places them in our path. But the frustration, the brokenheartedness, the suffering, the dispossession are all symptoms of something more basic. More important than relieving the symptoms, we have to treat the malady itself. As it is so often said, one does not have a cold because he sneezes but sneezes because he has a cold. Similarly we can say of the society in which we live that it is not sinful because it segregates; rather it segregates because it is sinful. Segregation and discrimination is the sneeze, the symptom of the condition of a sick and sinful society.

And what is the sin? To force fellow citizens, because of the color of their skins or any other reason, to live in ghettos which breed hostility, bitterness, and crime is wrong. But this is symptomatic. To refuse to employ people on the basis of race can hardly be justified by any Christian standard, but this is not the real threat to Christian doctrine. To threaten, taunt, and jeer mothers who take their children to the schools to which they have been assigned by law is to demonstrate less than Christian love, and yet the segregationist can debate you to a stand-off if you make this your starting point. These are all humanitarian and egalitarian concerns that certainly lie within the province of Christian witness but which, taken alone, are not enough. The segregationist who is honest and who wants to remain loyal to the church has very clearly seen this point and has taken clever advantage of its weakness.

There is, however, something that neither the segregationist nor the integrationist have seen. In a real sense man is *not* the subject, the point of reference for his own well-being and happiness upon the earth. Neither the racist nor the person upon whom he casts indignity, the disinherited, Negro or white, the builder of houses or the rejected from houses, the employer or the one deprived of employment, the passer of legislation or the victim of repressive legislation, the murderer or the murdered— none of these is the true referent, the true subject. The only point of reference is God.

The sin, therefore, is that the whole issue of race is an effort to deny the sovereignty of God, to negate the absolute supremacy of God. Once a man has truly seen this truth he can no longer be a racist, nor can he any longer grovel in the agonies of self-pity. From that point on, the racist logic and desire for self-justification terrify him. As for the racist, he is now afraid to call any man unclean, to discriminate against any man, to stand in judgment over any group or individual or to set himself above any of God's human creatures. From the moment either the segregationist or the integrationist really accepts the absolute sovereignty of God, he is forever thereafter terrified to usurp that authority or claim any part of it for himself. And that is precisely what one does when he determines his pattern of behavior by classifications of race and class or thinks that God is obliged to conform reality to his notion of what ought to be.

Now, of course, many people who hold the segregationist position claim also to accept the doctrine of the sovereignty of God. Most of those within the church have certainly been exposed to it. It has been dinned into the church and Christian society for two thousand years through the theologians from Paul to Augustine, Calvin, Barth, Niebuhr, and others. It is obvious, however, that the segregationists have not understood, for if they had, they would acknowledge that God, being truly supreme, could create as he saw fit, and that he did not create a hierarchy of man. The segregationist who uses Scripture to buttress segregation convicts himself at this very point. In not one of the passages he uses is there any record of the alteration of creation subsequent to the time God made man in his image. God did not intervene to alter creation until the appearance of the new creation in Jesus Christ and in the Kingdom of Christ categories and classification by color and race do not exist. It is worth noting that over most of the generations of Christians this truth was clearly perceived. Racism, as we know it today, is a modern development. C. Vann Woodward traces the development of Jim Crow legislation in his book *The Strange Career of Jim Crow* to show that restrictive statutes that are taken for granted today would have been considered completely unwarranted in the United States before 1900. Racism as a doctrine and a way of life was little known before the rise of the modern nation-state on the continent of Europe. In this country, the historical and sociological developments that helped make Jim Crow possible were preceded by a theological development that really evolved in the matrix of the whole history of Christianity in America.

The theological aspect of racism has its roots in the shift from incarnation to deification in Christian belief—

the shift in emphasis from God become man to man become God. F. O. Matthiessen has pointed out this inver-
sion in his treatment of the American renaissance when
he writes: "Anyone concerned with orthodoxy holds that
the spiritual decadence of the nineteenth century can be
measured according to the alteration in the object of its
belief from God-Man to Man-God" (*American Renaissance,* Oxford University Press, 1941, p. 446). Matthiessen understands this as a shift from belief in the salvation of man through the mercy and grace of a sovereign
God, to belief in the potential divinity in every man. In
no country was this theological development more rapid
than in Protestant, democratic America. The preaching of
the early church concerned a God who had become man,
a Christ whose birth was unique and whose nature was
divine; who was crucified and who died back into eternal
life. Theological liberalism particularly second-generation
liberalism, within Protestantism interpreted Jesus as a
rebel prophet who was murdered by a society that was
unable to abide the horror of truth. Accordingly, man
became God. Thus God was no longer incarnate in the
person of Christ. He did not become man by being
"in Christ"; rather, the man Jesus became God. (*Ibid.*)
In this formulation Christ did not descend from the
right hand of God to be born of a virgin, to suffer
under Pontius Pilate, to be crucified for us men and for
our salvation. In fact, this position does not really admit
of the incarnation. Jesus was thrust by man to the right
hand of God as a reward for the life he had lived and
the deeds he had performed. This was, in short, deification.

It is evident that the meaning of the crucifixion and
death of Christ is completely changed by this theology.
One of its most serious consequences is the rejection of
the doctrine of the absolute sovereignty of God, and it is
precisely this that has had far-reaching implications in

the whole field of Christian social relations. It is not difficult to see why this is so. The deification of Jesus was the
celebration of man's triumph, whereas God "in Christ"
(incarnation) had to do only with the sovereignty of God.
It has to do with what God had done by his sovereign
power. Protestant, democratic America could move easily
from this man-centered religion to the belief that nothing
was more important than the individual. It would be expected, therefore, that Protestant leaders, under this theological influence and bound by the spell of the American
creed of individual rights, would tackle the problem of
racial prejudice from this vantage point. With the dimi-
nution of the idea that man might find completion in
something greater than himself, what could follow more
naturally than for Protestantism to make man the subject
of racial and social justice? With man rather than God as
the subject, the motivation for human brotherhood was
lodged firmly in humanitarianism and man's need. What
now impels the seeker for justice? Often it is that drive,
that urge to "go about doing good" in order that the spark
of divinity in every man might shine forth.

With God as sovereign (subject), the basis for human
brotherhood is, as Matthiessen suggested, "in men's common aspiration and fallibility, in their humility before
God" (ibid., see p. 72). When man is the subject of social action and when humanitarianism is its motivation,
we are all too likely to badger people into loving each
other, to tell them that men are good and worthy and,
accordingly, there should be no discrimination among
them. The segregationist counters with facts and figures
about some men, the behavior of whom deserves, by our
standards of goodness and worthiness, only a second-class
citizenship. It is not sufficient to question his facts. Although he may not, for the most part, take into account
basic causes for the behavior he describes, his facts are
often quite accurate. But our argument does not rest upon

factuality. If God is sovereign, if the basis of our brother-hood is in our common frailty and humility before the One who "has made everything for its purpose, even the wicked for the day of trouble" (Prov. 16:4), then the statistical data of the segregationist, accurate or not, are of no account. They must be rejected as the basis of Christian decision.

The second generation of theological liberalism in the social gospel movement probably did more to impede progress in race relations in America by keeping man at the center of thought and action than did even funda-mentalism, which, though often a caricature of orthodoxy, contained more incarnation and less deification than liber-alism. This is not to "beat a dead horse to death." A dis-cussion of the social gospel movement is appropriate at this point in history only because the ethics of that move-ment persist (where race relations is concerned) even though the ghost of its theology has for the most part dis-appeared. How familiar at Christian race relations confer-ences are words of law and order, constitutional process, democracy, human dignity, and the rights of man! And how strange and out of place seems talk of "God in Christ," of incarnation, and of the mystical body when applied to social problems! And the person who is known for his Biblical preaching, who takes seriously the creeds and has a reputation for being "a good churchman," is not ex-pected to involve himself in the social crises of his day, and if he does, his "churchmanship" becomes just a bit suspect.

Racist logic is primarily concerned with what man thinks about man. Sometimes, either as a technique to influence those who *must* have God on their side, or as a result of his own misguided piety, his doctrine speaks of that which man, usually himself thinks about God. The Biblical writers, on the other hand, as Karl Barth has so often pointed out, were concerned with what God thinks about man. Their account makes God the subject and man the object. Their point of reference was God. When one is able and willing to confess that sovereignty belongs to God alone he is no longer able to be at ease in the camp of the racist. He ceases to be excessively preoccupied with man or with any particular man or group of men.

"It is he who sits above the circle of the earth. . . . who brings princes to nought, and makes the rulers of the earth as nothing. . . . He blows upon them, and they wither, and the tempest carries them off like stubble." (Isa. 40:22–24.) Isaiah's words now define the true center of human thought.

The Christian can now see that all his stereotypes about groups, even when true, have no real significance, for, again with Isaiah, he perceives that the inhabitants of the earth are as grasshoppers, and the folly of a quarrel between the Acridiidae family and the Locustidae family. The fact of having a Negro neighbor or shop foreman fades in importance when God becomes the center of thought and life and one acknowledges his absolute rule, authority, and government. There is no exception from this theological principle. The sovereignty of God means simply: "Know therefore this day, and lay it to your heart, that the Lord is God in heaven above and on the earth beneath; there is no other. . . . See now that I, even I, am he, and there is no god beside me; I kill and I make alive; I wound and I heal; and there is none that can deliver out of my hand" (Deut. 4:39; 32:39).

This, then, is the sovereignty of God. It is the beginning and the end of Christian race relations. It is only by beginning with God that we get a true perspective for the understanding of man. It is precisely this understanding of the nature of man that comprises the content of Christian race relations. Are some men different? Did God have intrinsic differences in mind when he created some men white and some colored? The priority of God's sov-

ereignty is what Calvin is driving at when he explains
that when we begin with ourselves rather than with God,
we see ourselves in a more powerful, glamorous, and impressive light than we actually are. To see ourselves as we
really are, we must begin with God. Otherwise the picture is distorted and what is presented to us is the image
of a creature who has the right to dispose of his fellow
men as he sees fit.

One cannot look God in the face without getting a
painful exposure to man's frailty and finiteness. We cannot look at God without "the shock of cemeteries." And a
casual glance at these ubiquitous abodes of those gone before reminds us of the simple truth with which both the
Bible and secular history are filled—that life is suffering
and sorrow and the beginning of death; that we all come
forth like a flower and are cut down; that we are all of a
few days and full of trouble; that all flesh is grass and we
are all here dying together. What man can face this truth
and continue to see the relevance of human classifications
of people into colors and races? What man can continue
to prate such "Bible belt" absurdities as "God was the original segregationist." When we confess God as Creator and
Sovereign who not only brought the world into being but
continues to be its sole sustainer and judge, we see that
no matter how high man may rise, no matter what legislation he may engineer, no matter how loudly he screams
"nigger, jew, dago, kike," his final outcome will be that of
the mighty kings of Judah, in the books of the Chronicles
and the Kings—Jehoahaz, Joash, Jeroboam. Each died
and slept with his fathers and another reigned in his stead
until he too died and slept with his fathers and another
took his vacant throne. To recognize God as Sovereign,
Creator, Judge, and Ruler of the universe is to see how
weak is the hand of men who must die and sleep with
their fathers and go down into the great sepulcher of the
earth together with "all sorts and conditions of men" only

to be raised and judged by that one Sovereign who is Lord of all.

So it is that the sin of the children of light has not been their failure to tell the world that "red and yellow, black or white, they are precious in his sight." That has been said sweetly and often enough. Our problem is that we have spoken too much of man's worth and dignity and not often enough of his insignificance in God's scheme of things. Sermons on race relations like to use the text from The Acts: "He made from one . . ." The favorite rejoinder of the segregationist has been the rest of the verse: ". . . having determined . . . the boundaries of their habitation" (Acts 17:26). Perhaps a more appropriate text for both would be from II Sam. 1:19: "How are the mighty fallen!" Here is a grim reminder for the potential self-righteousness of the integrationist and the vanity of the segregationist. "How are the mighty fallen!"

Thus far we have said little of the Lordship of Jesus Christ, which is the way the Christian must ultimately speak of God's sovereignty in this "time between," this "era of the church." It would appear, however, that today when the comfortable life of Americans deludes them into thinking that they have already achieved redemption one must speak more forcefully of creation, of finitude, and of sin. The doctrine of the sovereignty of God needs to fall afresh upon the ears of this generation. The God who is Sovereign has made Jesus "both Lord and Christ" (Acts 2:36). But before we can really understand what this means—before we can give up the illusions of the theology of everyman's deification, we must read again the Old Testament and stand under the judgment of Creation and Fall.

This is the note that must now be reintroduced into Christian race relations. It is found in both the Old Covenant and the New. "Thou art the God, thou alone, of all the kingdoms of the earth; thou hast made heaven and earth." (II Kings 19:15.) "I am the Alpha and the Omega, says the Lord God, who is and who was and who is to come, the Almighty." (Rev. 1:8.)

The Sovereign God who is our Lord Jesus Christ—he is the only subject, the sole referent of human relations and the social action of the church. What can be said of us, whatever our race or class, except that we and all our fortunes and destinies belong to him? And this is enough to know.

Chapter VI

Accomplishments and New Dangers

THE PICTURE WE HAVE PAINTED OF THE BEHAVIOR OF
the churches during the long, dark night of American
racism has not been a pretty and optimistic one. We do
not propose at this point to put it in a pastel frame. It is,
however, only fair to point out that although the churches
do not do the good they want, but the evil they do not
want is what they do (see Rom. 7:19), they are, nevertheless, doing more that is of long-lasting significance in
the field of race relations than any other institution of our
society. The churches can still be a decisive influence in
this struggle.

Robert Hutchins is reported to have said of the University of Chicago when he was its Chancellor: "It isn't
a very good school. It's just the best there is." The record
of the churches, as disappointing as it is, is not so bleak
when it is compared with the record of secular groups.

Before we can talk about what the church can do we
must look briefly at some of our limitations and at some
of the achievements of Protestant Christianity despite
those limitations. Of course, the term "Protestant Christianity" is so broad that anything claimed in its favor can
be refuted with numerous exceptions. One might ask:
"Which Protestants are you talking about? There are sixty
million Protestants in this country." And if we could an-

swer satisfactorily the question, "What are Protestants called to do?" we would have made a contribution which four hundred years of Protestant history has been unable to provide. For Protestantism has seldom been able to define clearly its role in society on any critical social issue, and in any given social crisis it is usually divided into warring factions.

The reasons for this have been suggested by various students of the relation of the Protestant churches to American culture. It has been pointed out that a major limitation the churches face is the manner in which Protestantism has divorced religious faith from institutionalized authority. The result has been that Protestantism does not recognize leaders who are authorized to speak the mind and will of the group. For example, all the major denominations have passed strong resolutions regarding racial segregation. Even though these statements have been approved by some authoritative body, there is no clearly delineated line of authority for implementation, for seldom is any person invested with sufficient power to act with anything like the immediacy necessary to make the church's declared policy effective in a crisis situation.

A second factor stressed by those in the field of the sociology of religion is that the excessive individualism of Protestantism gives every church member the right to interpret doctrine or Scripture as he sees fit. The consequence of such freedom is often conformity to values, prejudices, and attitudes acquired outside the church. Certainly there has been no dearth of positive statements by Protestant groups on the subject of race, but they are not taken seriously by legislatures and policy makers because it is well known that these statements only reflect the thinking being done at the highest level. At the grass roots, attitudes are apt to reflect that prevailing regional or community sentiment. Thus such denominational statements never quite comprise a clear threat to any individual or group of officials who retain power by election.

The painful awareness of this weakness is evident in the various ministerial statements and resolutions that have come out of communities in racial tension. There is always the preface that these clergymen, the signers, are speaking as individuals and not representing anyone particularly. This is not intended as a criticism of the individual minister who signs such statements. In a sense this is in his defense, for it is often to his peril that he signs antisegregation resolutions at all. But while the minister cannot speak for his constituency, other organizations with ideologies at variance with the Christian faith have developed, in a short time, clear channels of authority to speak convincingly to elected officials. Frequently these organizations speak for the same people for whom ministers or other church leaders are unable to speak, and they speak for those who would strongly object if the church or their councils sought to enunciate policy. A good example is the White Citizens' Councils or the John Birch Society. Christians within these groups generally resist any effort of their churches to represent them but strangely enough do not seem to object to having a small and powerful clique speak for them as members of those bodies. It is safe to say that people generally do not resent being represented if they share the adopted position. One can only conclude that while the official positions taken by Protestant bodies in various social crises may reflect a summation of the Law and the prophets, they are not a summation of the wishes of the majority of Protestant church members!

The point is that while Protestantism can and does plant seeds of revolution, it cannot see them through to fruition. To continue the struggle, its prophets and actionists often must turn to other vehicles. While it is true, however, that Protestant churches are not providing a leadership in race relations commensurate with the ideals and principles of Protestantism, it is equally true that they have produced many of the persons who *are* providing such leadership. Take a careful look at the reformers in the present crisis in race relations. Ask them where they got their start. Most of them will reply that it all began when they started to take seriously that which they had learned in religious training. We can be critical that Protestant polity has not provided the kind of organization necessary to influence social change, but we cannot ignore the fact that its doctrines and teachings, when taken seriously, have provided leaders for the groups that are organized for effective action.

Clarence Jordan is a Baptist minister who was one of the founders of Koinonia Farm in South Georgia. He holds a degree in agriculture and a Ph.D. in Greek from a theological seminary. Jordon organized the interracial farm from the coercion of a Christian conscience. Koinonia Farm has done much for Sumter County. It has introduced new agricultural techniques into the community and it has been a constant reminder to the world of the meaning of the word by which it is named. Because of his views and practices in race relations, Clarence Jordon was excluded from the Baptist church in which he held membership. We may be critical of that church for excluding such a good man from its fellowship, but we ought not to forget that it was that same institution which produced the good man in the first place. Like an eagle teaching its young to fly but deserting them once they begin to exercise what they have learned, so Protestantism is often capable of inspiring its own to action but almost as often rejects them when action occurs, especially if such action is taken in the name of the church. It is nothing new for Protestants who apply their faith to social, economic, and political problems to be told to mind their altar fires and tea parties. This restrictive policy is partly a consequence of the Reformation polity and doctrine of the church which left little room for institutionalized authority in its almost total rejection of Roman Catholicism.

Despite the fact that Protestant churches are not geared for action, some of the ablest leaders who *are* exerting the pressure for social change were nurtured by Protestant churches, even if they now deny the mother who gave them birth. Few of the people who are presently active in the struggle for racial justice have escaped the influence of the Judaeo-Christian ethic in one way or another. Indeed many of them have come disillusioned from the ranks of the Christian church itself—both Protestant and Catholic.

Much of what we have said in this book concerning the behavior of Protestantism in the racial crisis does not apply to Negro churchmen and Negro congregations. What follows here is not an attempt to exempt any group from its share of guilt. Rather, it is to single out some of the accomplishments of this particular wing of the church and suggest certain hazards that challenge the Negro churches.

No one can seriously question the role played thus far in the racial crisis by Negro clergymen and congregations. From Birmingham to Buffalo, Negro church buildings have served for years as centers of operation for groups working for racial justice, and ministers have usually served as their leaders. In part this has been redemptive. For, in view of this fact, no one can say categorically that Protestantism is making no worth-while contribution to the desegregation process. In Montgomery, Nashville, Atlanta, Detroit, Chicago, New York, Los Angeles, Negro Protestants have kept the pressure on, brought into being organized protest movements and undergone suffering and sacrifice to effect social change. Although it has been groups such as the National Association for the Advancement of Colored People which have played the major organizational role and have taken the giant legal steps, much of their leadership has come from within the churches. But in situations such as the Montgomery boycott and in many of the recent sit-in movements, it has been the institutional church itself that has made the greater contribution. Not only were the meetings held in church houses, but these meetings were essentially religious meetings in which religious values were dominant. The prayers, the refusal to return evil with evil, the agreement of ministers and laymen to accept imprisonment, the acceptance by entire communities of legal harassment and economic deprivation—these are things familiar to these people and it must be said that this was and is the church playing a vital role in the achievement of justice for all people.

It has often been said that the real key to the solution of our current problem of racism in America rests in the hands of the enlightened, liberal Negro churchmen, and not in the hands of white people—not even white people of good will. Actually it is strange that there should ever have been expected that white churchmen *could* be the real leaders of racial integration. Anyone even remotely familiar with community structure and organization, and, as we have seen, anyone acquainted with the Christian doctrine of man would not have entertained such a hope.

The role of Negro churchmen in keeping the pressure constantly upon the status quo is a vital one. In every case desegregation has not come when a group of whites of good will gathered and said discrimination was wrong and should be stopped. Rather, it has come when a group of Negroes gathered and said: "We have been discriminated against long enough. Let's stop it." This has been true in the schools of the South, and it has been equally true of housing, employment, and church membership in the North. There can be no minimizing the action-oriented witness of Negro churchmen. They have a distinct and unique role to play, and there is no denying that thus far they have played it more than well. But the point we shall now try to make has nothing to do with all that, as significant as it well may be.

What we need to see is that when God chooses people to do his work, it has nothing to do with the intrinsic merit of those he has called. The fact that God has summoned Negro churchmen to do his work in this crisis is not to their credit in the least. It has only to do with the Caller. It has nothing to do with the suffering of the chosen, the injustices wrought against them, the humiliation of being segregated as an inferior people, the inconvenience of discrimination. There is a clear parallel in the history of Israel. All these problems were also their problems. They too were for a time slaves, maltreated and humiliated. They too were chosen. But the choice had nothing to do with Israel. When the Children of Israel asserted their rights, as if rights gave them special merit and justification, there was nothing but trouble and violence from that moment. It was difficult to see what good could come from their struggles. The more they strove to be free, the more Pharaoh and the Egyptian majority caused them to suffer, and the more were arguments advanced against their freedom. But Moses, an outside agitator with no obvious business in Egypt but to make trouble, persisted. The "Uncle Toms" of Israel grumbled throughout it all. "Would that we had died . . . in the land of Egypt, when we sat by the fleshpots and ate bread to the full." (Ex. 16:3.) Pharaoh persisted in his policy through plagues of blood, frogs, gnats, flies, boils, ferocious weather, locusts, and darkness at noon—Little Rock hanging on through a plague of no much-needed new industry for two spiteful years; New Orleans with its loss of Mardi Gras revenues—refusing to give in.

The objective observer doubtless could see nothing but continued bitterness resulting from this kind of extreme recalcitrance. Certainly there were many moderates in the land who cautioned against the radical methods of the Jews. Israel won. Then lost. It won as long as the Israelites could see that they were chosen by a God whose aid in all their struggles proved nothing about themselves but only proved something about God—his supremacy, his sovereignty. Israel lost when the Israelites began to assume that all their afflictions and the favorable issue from them had to do with themselves. They lost whenever they believed that their being chosen had been for their own glory. The sin of the Children of Israel was not that they caused trouble for Egypt. This was inevitable. And what could have been more natural than to believe that as a people they were somehow favored because of their successes? But God had called them to establish his supremacy and not their own. The sin of Israel was their assumption that their calling had to do with their cause rather than with God's purposes.

If God has chosen Negro churchmen in this crisis, it is for the purpose of establishing to them, and to America, something about himself. The fact that Negroes are in the vanguard of the fight for justice must not lead anyone to think that they are less guilty of sin than any other group. Whenever people assert their rights, whether in this country or anywhere in the world, there is trouble. There are riots in Montgomery, arrests in Jackson, and panic in Leopoldville. The Negro, like Israel, is called to destroy the idols, to smash the images which we have erected and which have become more important to us than God himself. And when idols fall, there is always trouble and violence. It is foolish to derogate those who seek redress and to blame them for ensuing violence and trouble. It is, however, the better part of wisdom to sound a warning. In the struggle for righteousness, God's righteousness and God's purposes are the true meaning of the struggle. Here again it is not a matter of democracy, a man's rights, of constitution, of the Supreme Court. It is what God is able to do with sinful people and with sinful instruments to draw attention to himself and his purposes of redemption that matters.

In the various movements led by the Negro churches there is serious need for theological depth. Many of these efforts being made by churchmen and presumably in the name of Christ are more humanistic than Christocentric. It is interesting, for example, to note the degree to which the name of Mahatma Gandhi is invoked in the literature of the desegregation campaigns. The entire nonviolent movement is built much more around the teachings of the great Indian leader than around the teachings of Jesus Christ. This despite the fact that Negro Americans, like all other Americans, have been more exposed to Christian doctrine than to the Gandhian philosophy and despite the fact that a rationale for nonviolence has traditionally been derived from the life and teachings of Jesus Christ.

That Gandhi has been so widely used in this movement may reflect the Negro's subconscious rejection of Christianity as the white man's religion. The rapidly growing Black Muslim movement states this in unequivocal terms as a major reason for repudiation of Christianity. It is certainly understandable that the Negro has begun to look to other religions for spiritual substance to undergird his struggle for freedom. The danger is that the Christian church seems to offer nothing more than its institutional form as a vehicle to accomplish ends motivated by an alien philosophy.

It is nonetheless true that if there is to be real renewal of the church in our century it is possible that it will be achieved through the predominantly Negro communions, especially if there is no drastic change from their comfort-loving, status-ridden complacencies by white Protestantism. It has always been that a suffering people seem to respond more readily to the call of God.

But again the danger is that the response to the call

will not be a true "covenanting" with God. It is a false idea of covenant to say to God: "If you will deliver us out of our afflictions we will be your people." This is not what a covenant relationship means. If Negro churchmen in America can see the covenant only as the privilege of serving God and living in communion with him, aware all the while of the dangerous condition of being a special agent of his holy concern, if they see man's role in the covenant as the acknowledgment of the unconditional sovereignty of the Ruler of the nations, then there is hope that Christianity will survive this period of testing. But if Negro churchmen begin to assume that on the basis of the covenant they are entitled to claim selfish rights before God and to be dealt with in some favored manner that accords with their own notion of what is good for them, there will not be a renewal of the church through them. The word "covenant" does not mean a bilateral contract between two equal parties. This was precisely Israel's sin. It is cause for alarm to hear repeatedly at freedom rallies: "*We* are going to win because God is on *our* side!" This is assumed in every revolution. It was assumed in the American Revolution, but what happened? "Jeshurun waxed fat, and kicked; . . . then he forsook God who made him, and scoffed at the Rock of his salvation." (Deut. 32:15.)

The freedom movements working within the churches are, to some extent, the victims of the same theological shift mentioned earlier. They have tended to forget that there is something more at stake than the satisfaction of the individual, that man must find completion in One who is greater than himself, that the real basis for brotherhood is not humanitarianism but our common fallibility before God. The indignities the Negro has known, the injustices he has endured, are a sin against God on the part of the majority, and the sour grapes we have eaten will set our children's teeth on edge for generations to come. The struggle for freedom should not, must not, and will not be stopped. But let us not permit the successes that are now evident to tempt us to be prideful. Let the warning be sounded that the victors, to their despair, often come to accept the gods of the vanquished. In so far as that god is not the God and Father of Jesus Christ, let the Freedom Movement and the rising Negro middle class that will gain momentum by its victory test the spirits which impel their forward march. God has called and is yet calling the Negro churches to be the source of renewal for the whole church of Christ. Upon their understanding of the true meaning of the struggle for racial justice hangs the possibility of the church seizing or missing the opportunity God holds out to it in this generation.

Chapter VII

The Church: Prophet and Conservator

THERE ARE MANY THINGS THE CHURCH MIGHT HAVE done in the racial crisis. Modern prophets could have thundered from thousands of pulpits against the sin of segregation and injustice. The church could have given more time to the proclamation that in the sight of God there is no difference between black and white. The church could have led the attack on racism, first of all, by throwing wide its own doors to the Negro. These things a truly prophetic church would have done, but there is little to be gained by weeping for what might have been. There is still time for faithfulness. There is yet a chance for the church, if indeed we are still the church, to find its life, to be renewed. But if it happens, it will be God's doing and not ours.

We have said that many religiously motivated people cannot find a channel within the institutional church to express the social implications of their faith. But Protestantism does not hold that the Sunday morning expression of the church is the only type of the beloved community. Protestantism is free to encourage a congregation to find expression in groups geared to accomplish their own purposes in mission. In a sense it is tragic that Christians seem obliged today to go outside the framework of the church to bear witness. Nevertheless, such a witness is valid and efforts to relate faith to secular action groups cannot be dismissed as outside the pale of Christian social action. It should, however, be acknowledged that more and more Protestants are finding it possible to work within the structure of the church. In one city, a congregation rejected the gift of a valuable building site rather than compromise its conviction on man's unity in God. In another community, an entire congregation endorsed a nonchurch committee that had been formed to try to reopen the public schools. Such instances are still exceptional, however. More often it will be found that *individuals* are doing something, but that there is no concerted action by a congregation. One man is not a church. At the same time, we must not underestimate the significance of the statements condemning segregation that have been released by the major denominations. While such pronouncements do not ordinarily impress political leaders, they often give leverage to the local minister who faces congregational opposition in his efforts to be faithful to the gospel.

Another obligation that many Protestants are beginning to accept is the correction of the flagrant misuse of Scripture by segregationists. For some years Protestant leaders assumed that people were not being influenced by the spurious use of certain Bible passages which appear to support racial prejudice. Some leaders considered it boorish and unsophisticated to fight over proof texts and certainly not at the level that many of the segregationists had pitched the battle. It has now become obvious that the segregationist Protestant is neither rationalizing nor deliberately deceiving when he cites what he thinks is Scriptural authority for his convictions. God became the original segregationist, he argues, when he turned some of Noah's children black. And did not Jesus teach in the Golden Rule that we were not to do unto others what we would not want them to do to us? "Therefore," continues the segregationist, "since I don't want others to force me to integrate, it is my Christian duty to see that no one else is forced to integrate."

To point out that these arguments are illogical and false is not enough. This man is usually incapable of grasping the meaning of mythic context of some of the Biblical literature and often he may be unable even to read the text correctly. We must remember the educational level of those who are the most ardent antagonists and keep in mind the constant flow of low grade emotionally inflammatory literature that goes into the R.F.D. mailboxes. The only answer that will have meaning for these people is a steady refutation of segregation by citing chapter and verse. Even this may not succeed, but it appears to hold out the best promise for the present.

Still another role that Protestants are assuming is the support of those clergy and laymen who have dared to put their faith into action whatever the cost. Several denominations and groups as the National Council of Churches, American Friends Service Committee, United Presbyterian Church, the American Baptist Convention, and the United Church of Christ social action units have provided financial and other assistance to numerous individuals who have been displaced or have suffered in bringing the imperatives of their faith to bear upon the racial crisis. Certain congregations that have experienced financial loss because of their witness have also been aided by these agencies. We cannot, however, overlook the possibility of a grave danger in this policy. Consider the case of the local pastor who is warned by his denominational executive not to move too fast in the face of controversy lest there be a decline in membership or giving. When the pastor heeds the warning and his ministry flourishes in measurable terms, his ecclesiastical superior is apt to point out to him that God has blessed his cautious efforts and that it pays to serve Jesus in this way.

But let us suppose the pastor is troubled by this and

seeks to prove to his superior that one can be daring in his witness and still meet his denominational quotas. Unfortunately it is true that this cannot always be done, and when a minister launches out into the deep of controversy he may discover that it does *not* pay to serve his Lord. Quotas are not met, the number of tithers decline, and the institutional structure *does* sag. It is at this point that we are tempted to come to the pastor's support to prove to the bishop or the presbytery that God will in a material way bless a strong witness in social relations. We try to protect the man from suffering and to shield his church from organizational failure. But is this consistent with the Christian understanding of evil and the necessities of faithful obedience? The Christian who does battle with the devil, the powers, the world rulers of this present darkness, will undoubtedly suffer. But often such suffering is redemptive. When we try to mitigate the suffering, to prop up the faltering institution, and to insist that one can fight the world and the devil without suffering, we are denying a fundamental truth of Christian history and moral experience.

In any case, the denominations, even though the prophetic voice at the congregational level has been disappearing from long disuse, have begun, however haltingly, to act with effect. And it is high time, for the issue of racial injustice is nationwide and must be fought on a wide front by the national denominations as well as local congregations. Apart from schools and places of public accommodation, it is difficult to distinguish between the treatment of Negroes in Dothan, Alabama, and Montpelier, Vermont. A Negro looking for a house might easily have more trouble in suburban Philadelphia than in suburban Birmingham. A Jewish doctor might well be better received by the community in Vicksburg, Mississippi, than in Aberdeen, South Dakota.

Throughout the world racial bitterness, suspicion, and

mistrust is poisoning community life. The Black Muslims flourish among Negro Americans and represent much more than the impulsive passions of a few hotheads. The resurgence of the Klan and the rapid growth of the White Citizens' Councils are not merely a manifestation of Southern die-hardism. This feeling shows up all over the land—in Levittown, Dearborn, Deerfield Park, Little Rock, Sylacauga, Fayette County. Everywhere man in his sin thinks more highly of himself than he ought and finds it convenient to regard himself different from and superior to his fellows. Everywhere men categorize and classify one another. Everywhere race, color, class, religion, nationality tear men asunder. One cannot read a major daily paper anywhere in the world without finding at least one front-page story with racial and ethnic overtones— from South Africa to the Soviet Union, from England to the Congo, from Little Rock to Westchester County. Apart from the contest between communism and democracy, the struggle between the races, between the white and the colored peoples of the world, is the most deep-seated and perplexing problem of our time. We are in the midst of a revolution. Make no mistake about that. People of color will not halt in their drive for freedom. You can hear their song throughout the world, and it will not be silenced. It is the plainsong of the oppressed, the chant of the disinherited. "Free-dum. Free-dum." The passive and gentle bus rider in Alabama sings it as an anthem of praise; the restless and turbulent Congolese shouts it as a marching song. Neither will be stopped. Nor will the overarching seriousness of the East-West struggle and its eventual outcome silence the challenge that has been thrown down to the white man all over the world.

These people will be frustrated again and again by the Verwoerds, the Eastlands, the Kaspers, and the Levitts, but they will not be stopped. Man, by nature, does not give up privilege and comfort, status and security, without a struggle. At the same time, man does not cease to yearn for freedom. All of us are caught between these forces, whether we are innocent victims or calculating participants. It is evident that we will experience an extended social convulsion—a generation, perhaps more, of racial disharmony.

But the church has in the past found spiritual renewal in just such a day as this. It has found renewal because it rediscovered its purpose, or perhaps because God, in such a day, chooses to exert his purpose. This can be a time of greatness for the church, its hour of faithful obedience to the Word of God. And yet even without the full measure of obedience God can use the church to serve his purpose. This truth should not make us lessen our effort, but it has always been so. It may be that in our day God will use the church in quite a different way than those of us who have been on the battle line have hoped.

The church has always had two edges—a prophetic or pioneering edge and a stabilizing or conserving edge. Critics of the church usually see its conservative nature as the church's greatest weakness. In the present crisis in race relations this side of the church may become its strength and the source of the only important contribution the church may make.

Where civil disorder and commotion hold sway, where there is violence and strife, there is one role which the church has played well and may play with real effect in the future. This is what we may call by the rather unlovely term "cleaning up the mess." There is no better way to put what must, in all events, be done, and what the church perhaps is able to do best. Generally speaking, white Protestantism cannot be expected to play an active role in getting Negro children into all-white schools, in breaking up ghettos and admitting Negroes and Jews to previously restricted neighborhoods, in carrying the full brunt of the fight for employment on a fair and nondiscriminatory basis. White Protestantism could do these things, but it will not. It will not engage in the rough-and-tumble of politics to force civil rights cases through the courts. It has usually and it may be expected to continue to act in the interest of peace, harmony, good will, and order within the fellowship of its members. As social institutions, white Protestant churches are by nature conservative.

Moreover, based on past performance, there is little likelihood that white Protestantism will play any significant role in preparing communities for true integration or even desegregation. This is not to minimize the good work that has been done in some situations. It is simply to say once again that Protestantism is not geared for this kind of action and will not seek to exert the influence necessary for such preparation. We are *not* saying that is the way it should be and that we are happy about it. As the thrust for freedom becomes more radical in method with freedom rides, sit-ins, jail-ins, the action of the churches becomes more irrelevant. The Protestant social action professional was considered a radical by the end of 1959. Today he is hardly considered a liberal by the new movements for desegregation. If Protestant social action does not shift its tactics for any other reason, it needs a new strategy to justify calling itself by that name.

The task of "cleaning up the mess," if it comes to this, will be done well by the largely conservative Protestant denominations. For example, the churches in Clinton, Tennessee, played virtually no part in pressing for justice to admit Negro children to the public schools, and when they were admitted by court order they did little to prepare the community for an orderly transition. This was true to their conservative nature. A conservative institution seldom threatens another conservative institution. But when the whole structure of the community was falling apart, when cultural values even more sacred than racial views were threatened, that same conservative nature compelled the churches of Clinton to become involved. It was a "cleaning up," stabilizing, restoring job. For the churches to press for justice in court or community would be to jeopardize the success of revivals, membership drives, building funds, every member canvasses, and the whole life of the institution. But mob rule, riots, general hysteria, and bad publicity were an even greater threat. Decency had to be restored, and with it came some modicum of justice.

While a conservative institution will seldom threaten another conservative institution, it will almost always defend one. Thus, it was not that the Baptist church in Clinton had moved to a more liberal position when it supported its minister who walked to school with the Negro children and was attacked by the mob. Instead, this was a clear demonstration and re-emphasis of its continued conservatism. If their pastor had been beaten while circulating a petition to admit Negro children to the schools, he probably would have been dismissed from his pulpit. Agitation by petition would have been a betrayal of the peace-loving nature of the church. But when he was beaten in what amounted to the defense of a still more important community value—peace and stability—he became something of a Christian hero. The conservative nature of the institution had not changed. The identification of the enemy had.

Thus, white Protestant churches can be counted upon to play a vital role when the walls of civilization are caving in around them. In view of events, it must be admitted that this "caving in" is one phase of the process that we are observing today in most communities and nations where the race problem exists. Whether it takes the violent form of the crisis in the Congo or the one in Southern United States, or the more subtle—though always potentially violent—developments in Harlem, Dearborn, or Chicago, the result is largely the same. There are prophets within the Protestant fold who would like to see the church plug the dike with its right arm. Most of Protestantism is not willing to do this, but it is at least willing to rescue the drowning victims. And this much is not lightly to be dismissed.

Most Protestants will agree that the judgment and justice of God must precede any real reconciliation. They can avoid any doctrinal inconsistency by acknowledging that judgment and justice must come through channels other than the church—the NAACP, the courts, the President's Committee on Employment Opportunity—accepting as the church's role the mending of a broken and shattered society, the putting of the pieces back together in some kind of order, the cleaning up of the mess. Some of us will doubtless argue that this falls far short of the ideals for which the church should stand and that such a "let John do it" attitude can be given no room in the faith. Both of these things are true. But we are a selfish people and God has used selfish motivations before, and he may use again our selfishness for his own glory. This is precisely the point I wish to make. The church may be renewed in spite of man. God may take our greed and ambition, our fondness for the status quo, our desire for bigness and success, our concern for membership statistics, and use them in a manner we could never have imagined.

If God permits the church to play the role of putting the pieces back together because we love harmony and order, that does not mean that he has removed from his church the responsibility for bearing a prophetic and pioneering witness. It is only to say that this is the last chance. And if we are *content* with this, if it does not trouble us, we are in real trouble. But it is only recognizing what God can do with our faithfulness, our fears, and our weak motivation.

If the church does well this task of putting the pieces back together, it will have served its Lord despite itself; and it may even find its life. But let us be quite clear. Even so, the church must become, or allow itself to become, something it now is not. If we are looking for something the church can do and still hold on to the success and glamour of the institution, even the conserving, restoring role must be rejected. This role can be performed only at great risk and sacrifice. This is a skin graft; the operation is painful and hazardous to both patients. I am not suggesting this task as a way for the church to salve its conscience and still maintain the status quo. The church must be a haven for those weary of the battle. It cannot be just another pot in which to stew and boil. It must be the third race, the people of God, not the stiff-necked people of the culture.

When the church was young and yet without a name, a descriptive title given to it by some outsiders was "the people who love one another." Whether or not this was a derisive cognomen is not clear. But the world today uses it in jest and has turned it into an epithet. It asks, "Where are the people who *claim* to love one another?"

The church began as the people of God. The measuring rod by which Christians tested themselves in the "new creation" was whether or not they had love one for the other. "We know that we have passed out of death into life, because we love the brethren." (I John 3:14.) These people loved one another because they knew the tragedy of human existence and in their common frailty they saw the greatness and sovereignty of God. And the only *raison d'etre* of the people of God was and is the service of God. Therefore, before we can begin the task of mending the broken bits of society, our own humpty-dumptiness must be considered and remedied. We can deceive neither God nor ourselves. We cannot for long make ourselves believe that there are certain rights and privileges which he has ordained for some of us and denied to others because of race. But as long as we languish in this sin we can only hope that God will take our selfish motives and enlarge his love for the world by using us to mend its wounds.

Already there are signs of an ill wind blowing some good. One of the highlights of my experience during the past five years in a ministry that has taken me into every major racial crisis in the nation was to be a part of an interracial conference held in the Deep South for the purpose of discussing race relations. At the conclusion of the conference we knelt at the Lord's Table in a Methodist chapel in a Communion service following the order of the Presbyterian Church. The service was conducted by a white Congregationalist and a Negro Baptist minister. Kneeling together were Baptists, Episcopalians, Methodists, Presbyterians, and members of other communions, without thought of race.

This was no meeting for general fellowship. There were problems that had to be settled, but I know of no other occasion that would have brought the group to partake of those holy mysteries in the spirit that prevailed in that chapel. When Christians are caught in a serious crisis they will sometimes transcend ecclesiastical structures and barriers. True ecumenicity at the grass roots might well be accomplished in a crisis long before it is achieved at the top level. This conference was held in the midst of a crisis —a crisis brought about by the weakness and ineptitude of institutionalized religion.

Another example of unity born, not out of the strength, but out of the weakness, of the church in this crisis is now being seen throughout the country. Its symbol is a little lapel pin worn by members of various Christian bodies who have committed themselves to an informal fellowship of penitence called simply "Brothers." There are no dues, no membership roll, no officers. A group of individuals wear the pin and carry in their pocket a card which pledges them to remember at Mass, Holy Communion, quiet hours, worship services, and in their private devotions the brokenness of Christ's body because of racial divisions.

If one inquires what the pin means, the "Brother" shows his card which explains the fellowship. If someone expresses an interest, he is given the pin and card and the Brother writes for another. He may secure another set from one of four addresses, all of them the offices of men who give their time and effort to the healing of racial division. One of these addresses is that of a Roman Catholic organization. Another is the address of an unofficial denominational office. A third is the location of a Protestant Council field office. The last is a local church. No one anticipates in this an early union of Rome, Canterbury, and the rest of Christendom, but at least members of the separate branches of the holy catholic church at the unofficial and local level are being brought by the racial crisis to a recognition of the existence of each other.

Still another case of ecumenicity that is a result of the racial crisis (really the crisis of the church) is a group of theological students who call themselves "The Student Interracial Ministry." These young men and women come from all over the country and are attending seminaries in New York, Atlanta, Washington, Nashville, and other cities. White students spend one or more summers as assistant pastors in Negro congregations. Negro seminarians do the same in white congregations. Denomination is not a factor. Race is, but only in order that race may someday cease to be a factor in the church of Christ. The broken body of our Lord may yet be healed because God is moving us to heal our own racial divisions in such movements as these.

The churches are discovering many practical ways of helping their fellow Christians who are caught in the throes of racial upheaval. But we must be willing to use no gimmicks, no program kits. The only way we can minister to a man is to go with him. In the words of Barak to Deborah when he was assigned an almost impossible task: "If you will go with me I will go; but if you will not go with me I will not go" (Judges 4:8). More and more we see Christians, clergy and lay, "going with" fellow Christians, minority and majority alike. If he must suffer, we must suffer with him. If after our Gethsemane together there must still be Calvary, we must go as far as we can go together. And many are finding in this crisis that though Gethsemane preceded Golgotha, it did not take its place.

The early church did not exist in utopia. Neither did it have the notion we seem to have today, that if it could somehow change the society in which it existed into a sea of tolerance and brotherly love then it could truly be the church. It is dishonest and cowardly to assume that if we can make culture into what the church wishes it to be but isn't, the church can then be what it ought to be. The church will not regain its health when it is able to influence society to desegregate the many aspects of its life. Originally it was *because* of the brokenness, the misery of society, that the church could have any identification, any existence at all. We may be living in such a time.

As significant as the prophetic edge of the church is, and as much as most of us regret the present dearth of prophets in the land, it may well be that heroic deeds will come, not by the appearance of more and greater prophets, but as God uses the conserving edge which is, from our point of view, the weakness of the church. Making the conscious decision to play the conserving role and put our house in order is far from what the church might fairly have been expected to do. And if even this much is done it is not something of which we can boast, for it will have been that which God has done through us and often despite ourselves. And if it is done, the Kingdom will not have come, only the starting point will have been reached—that which was established at Pentecost concerning race will have been realized.

If we must despair of man, let us not despair of God. If God accepts the church with its selfishness, its fears, its obsession with peace and prosperity, and uses it once again as the channel of his grace, then we can at least know that this beleaguered church still belongs to him and he has not despaired of man.

Questions for Study and Discussion

Chapter I. Are *We* Still the Church?

1. Was the Supreme Court decision on segregation in the schools essentially a legal and sociological decision or essentially a religious decision? Is it possible to say that this decision was based on moral law to which the churches have borne a constant witness?

2. It is true, as the author suggests on page 6, that it is the nature of man to be vindictive as a consequence of oppression and exploitation?

3. It has been said, and the author gives supporting Biblical evidence, that "Christianity creates its own culture." How would you evaluate this contention?

4. Many people, not all expressly segregationist, have argued that people *prefer* to go to churches of their own color. To what degree is this true or false?

5. Does the church cease being the church when it refuses to admit persons of a minority group? What are the marks of a true church or the requisite factor which makes a church false?

Chapter II. The Nature of the Problem

1. To what extent must one differentiate between the Black Muslim movement and the National Association for the Advancement of Colored People? Can they be lumped together as racist? Further, are there significant differ-

ences between the NAACP and the White Citizens' Councils?

2. The author speaks of dormant racial prejudice in the North. Is this accurate, or would this be better designated as class or economic group prejudice?

3. What is, if any, the linkage between political conservatism and the doctrine of racial segregation? What does the John Birch Society stand for, and what should be the attitude of the church toward it?

4. What do you think of the author's refutation of the segregationist's argument from Genesis? Does the account of Creation really support a doctrine of racial assimilation?

5. What is our responsibility as Christians to friends who say that they cannot, in good conscience, acknowledge the rightness of racial integration?

Chapter III. The Gods of Law and Order

1. The question of civil disobedience has come to the fore again in this country through the campaigns in the South of the sit-in movements. Is the Christian justified in disobeying the law when he believes such laws conflict with his religious convictions?

2. The author admits that the social sciences, law, and humanitarianism "have a place in the church . . . but . . ." (page 32). Do you agree with his understanding of their role? To what extent does the gospel transcend these "human agencies"?

3. Should Christian parents be willing to sacrifice the peaceful social adjustment of their child in school for the "radical faithfulness" of Abraham by enrolling the child in a school seething with racial tension? What does God expect from us in such moments of decision? What is the responsibility of the whole church, rather than individual parents, in such situations?

Chapter IV. The Humanistic Detour

1. Do you agree that the church has no right to criticize segregation and discrimination in secular society until it has

desegregated its own local congregations and church agencies?

2. What do you think of the author's approach to the segregationist Christian? If you grant its theological validity, would you also grant its realism and effectiveness? Should the two be considered mutually exclusive? Are we concerned with "success" in the struggle for racial justice and the racially inclusive church?

3. The author insists that compassion in race relations is the wrong attitude with which to begin. Do you agree? Did Jesus regard men first with compassion or was he first concerned with their sin and alienation from God? What should be the basic motivation of the church today?

4. How should the church respond to economic reprisals like those imposed upon the Negro farmers of Fayette County, Tennessee? In some areas Negro Christians have retaliated with economic boycott of white merchants. Is the boycott a legitimate means of Christian action?

5. Do you think that pronouncement of the judgment of God is an effective means of making the modern American become aware of his sin? How is it received by people who are not members of the church? How can it be communicated with contemporary relevance?

Chapter V. The Christian Concern and Starting Point

1. What are the dangers of a "monolithic ecclesiastical structure" in the Protestant churches today? Is the loss of some democratic privileges in the church a reasonable and necessary price to pay for an effective social witness?

2. How is the doctrine of God's sovereignty related to human brotherhood? Campbell contends that Christian race relations begins with this emphasis. Do you agree? What teaching of the church seems to you more basic?

3. Is the dignity and worth of the human personality a Christian doctrine? What are the dangers of an excessive emphasis upon man, his needs, his rights and privileges? Is it too much to assume that oppressed groups will understand the idolatry of basing the struggle for justice upon anything other than God's sovereign will to turn men from their own needs to his judgment and mercy?

Chapter VI. Accomplishments and New Dangers

1. How much should a pastor undertake an active witness in race relations without the official support of his congregation? Is it feasible for the General Assembly of the church to move out in race relations and other social questions beyond the attitude and commitment of the churches?

2. Is it enough for the church to send leaders in the struggle for justice into secular organizations to carry on the fight or should the church itself enter the struggle at the level of politics and direct action? Will this blunt the *religious* effectiveness of its ministry?

3. What should be the role of the Negro churches? Should the white churches encourage them to carry on the effort for racial justice and play a strong supporting role rather than pre-empt their right of initiation and leadership?

4. Do you consider the use of Gandhian philosophy a dangerous trend in the desegregation movements? Can Christianity use this philosophy and method for social change without losing its distinctive Christian orientation?

Chapter VII. The Church: Prophet and Conservator

1. What is the value of church public pronouncements in the area of race relations? Should local churches make them?

2. Should economic assistance be provided for clergymen who are under economic duress because of their stand on the race problem?

3. Is it too pessimistic a view of the contemporary church to assume that only its "conservative role" will be relevant to the present crisis in race relations? How would you modify this point of view as stated by Campbell.

4. What are the encouraging signs of the prophetic role and the renewal of the church in the movement for justice and human rights in your community? What can be done to strengthen this aspect of the church's witness? Is the "Brothers movement" a prophetic or conservative response?

5. Should the main burden of the church's witness be upon changing society or changing people in the church and healing denominational fragmentation in America?